BUILT IN BRITAIN

A CHANNEL FOUR BOOK

BUILT IN BRITAIN

Gillian Darley

Weidenfeld and Nicolson · London
in association with
Channel Four Television Company Limited

Half title page
*The gable end of Haunt Hill House, Great Weldon in
Northamptonshire*

Title page
Welsh barns at Taltreuddyn behind a dry-stone wall

The television series BUILT IN BRITAIN was produced
for Channel 4 by Artifax Limited.

First published in Great Britain by
George Weidenfeld and Nicolson Ltd
91 Clapham High St, London SW4 78A

Edited by Charyn Jones
Designed by Sally Smallwood

ISBN 0 297 78312 2

Colour separations by Newsele Litho Ltd.
Filmset by Butler and Tanner Ltd.
Printed and bound in Great Britain by Butler & Tanner Ltd,
Frome and London

Contents

Introduction

If you live in a city the view from your window is probably a dense, urban panorama. As I write this, I look out over London at houses of every hue of brick; red, grey, yellow, orange, brown. There are slate roofs, roofs of various coloured cement tiles, even a few of the older, tomato-red terracotta tiles. In the far distance, the buildings are of precast concrete and glass, with, it can be safely assumed, steel frames beneath. There are notable historic buildings too – St Paul's Cathedral, the Palace of Westminster and the Old Bailey – all architect-designed and built of the best materials available, brought long distances at great expense. The only gap in this representative slice of London, and many other major cities could offer a similar scene, is the absence of any buildings which illustrate the traditional link between the buildings and the site on which they stand. That category, in which architecture is the result of the skills and the materials of the locality, and the needs and wishes of the users, is known as vernacular architecture. It represents a dialect, a particular regional flavour and gives to each area a strongly individual character.

Almost every building in that view from my window is the product of an industrial society, which from the eighteenth century could fetch and carry its goods from wherever they could be obtained at the right price. If there are any relics of the timber-framed architecture that once was the vernacular of London, as in much of the south east of England, they are as rare as platinum and buried deep. The creations of the exceptionally wealthy patrons of architecture, from the medieval period onwards, are exceptions. With the emergence of the professional architect in the seventeenth century, the dividing line between the evolving traditional building skills and the fashion-conscious world of design in which Italy, France or ancient Rome set the style, became further accentuated. Careful study of ancient monuments or the reading of erudite publications were not the stuff of vernacular architecture. Professor R.W. Brunskill has distinguished between vernacular buildings and 'polite' architecture – that is the architecturally conversant designs of village parsonages or town halls of the early eighteenth century onwards which are the product of established pattern rather than native wisdom and example.

Where one category stops and the other starts is the stuff of much learned discussion, and remains unresolved. It is, perhaps, almost an instinctive distinction but with a proviso that revolutions in transport and industrial processes ended the era in which the local forests and quarries, fields and coastlines had provided the material for the buildings of the immediate area.

The buildings we see now in any given area provide a partial picture of vernacular architecture as it evolved from the sixteenth

The gable end of these cottages in Saffron Walden has patterned brickwork, known as nogging, filling in the panels between the studs. It was probably a later addition. The timber framing on the front is covered with plaster, which is decorated with pargetting.

6

century onwards. What is missing is that vast category of humble buildings which were constantly being replaced – the squatter huts of the landless labourers, the rudimentary barns and outbuildings that must have accompanied houses and cottages alike, and, of course, enormous numbers of farmhouses, barns, cottages or mills that have gone since the vernacular tradition died a century ago.

The eight brief essays in this book on relatively small, and in some cases, very tiny, geographical areas cannot do more than offer their flavour and some explanation for what constitutes the traditional built landscape of that particular district. The nature of the subject, the way in which men have chosen materials, developed techniques and skills, and the geological and climatic determinants with which they were faced, is to suggest a set of variations upon a theme. By choosing eight widely separated and very distinct parts of the British Isles, I hope that these differences are self evident.

Everybody who travels around England, Scotland and Wales has their favourite corners. With little difficulty another eight areas, equally distinct, equally intriguing, could be added to these. The buildings, far more than the academic exercises of leading architects or the pattern-book homogeneity of eighteenth- or nineteenth-century town housing, offer clues to the personalities and preferences of those who built them and those who used them. The trademark of a local carpenter or mason might be confined to a single valley or might never be found in districts beyond the range of one man's daily journey by horse and cart. There was, of course, plenty of borrowing too; you can trace features as they move across the country, south to north or from rich, accessible areas into remote mountain ranges. The process might take decades, it might even take centuries as economic parity was reached between those areas with natural advantages and those with disadvantages hard to surmount.

While in some respects vernacular architecture is about distinguishing marks, or particular preferences, in others it is about the common ground. The evolution of the domestic house plan, despite marked local variations such as where to place the main entrance or the principal chimney stack, follows a consistent path from the rudimentary single room to an ever more complex series of subdivisions between the space of four walls. Whether it was taking place in the north-western extremities of Wales or the Kentish Weald, in the sixteenth century or the fourteenth century, the impulses are comparable. The personal aspirations and daily habits of the user – merchant, farmer, miller or labourer – are the key. At the upper end of the social scale, the pattern was set, and over time and distance that example became the model, all the way through society. The power of conservatism on one hand and the desire to show-off on the other combined to produce some odd anachronisms in traditional buildings of the fifteenth and sixteenth centuries. For example, at one end of the country, in Devon, farmhouses kept their medieval open

An open-fronted hay barn on the coast near Harlech in Wales (left) and a thatched cob wall in Devon (right) demonstrate the combination of traditional skills and practicality.

The solid end walls of the hay barn are made up of boulders, while the open sides are supported on plinths of stone.

halls long after there was reason and precedent to floor them over. Similarly, at the northern end of the country, the Scottish tower house, complete with battlements on parapets, arrow slits and thick walls, lingered on even after increased stability had rendered their defensive design obsolete. These quirks, at odds with the practical approach in all other aspects of the vernacular builder, explain other apparently anomalous details in buildings whose look was almost wholly determined by their function.

Although domestic buildings are predominant in this study, and chiefly rural ones, the functional buildings that surrounded them are not ignored. The farmhouse was, of course, itself a functional building, with storage in the attics and a dairy, brew-house or smoking chambers within or next to the house itself. It is the often unaltered forms of barns and mills, granaries and oast houses which tell of traditional materials and functional forms. They characterise the landscape of particular areas as much as the farmhouses and cottages.

However, it is easy to be misled. Although we now, rightly, associate the Pennines with stone or North Norfolk with flint as indigenous building materials, in neither case were they used for the general run of building until the seventeenth century. Before that, as in Essex

Ornamentation is here used on the keystone to the arched entrance of a Pennines barn. The overhang, supported on stone brackets, is a touch of practicality, giving a measure of protection against the rain. Notice the random rubble walls and the detailed freestone of the arch itself.

Suffolk, or the Weald, timber and earth were the material of ordinary buildings, as opposed to ecclesiastical buildings, great houses or tithe barns. Only when the timber became scarce did local people look around and develop an alternative. Ready supply and traditional skills kept the old practices going until they were beaten. The transition between a vernacular building skill based on the finely balanced system of jointed timbers and that based upon the simple concept of heaped masonry – in effect on gravity – was considerable. Skills that developed over long generations in the carpentry business, nurtured by constant demand, died away. New skills, responsive to the qualities offered by fine freestone or even the resourcefulness of making the best of what came to hand, took their place and evolved. These were the processes of vernacular building; a pragmatic affair in which expediency and practicality were the guidelines.

Changes in form or materials in buildings today have much to do with regulations and marketing. It makes better sense to use concrete blocks and steel cladding and it is after all what we have all become used to; it is our vernacular. Now, as always, most people faced with the problem of building would not do anything wildly original; they echo what they already know, and like, and find workable and then, perhaps, add a personal touch of some kind as a distinguishing mark. Innovation remains the province of an exceptional imagination or bravura creativity: presumably the new developments in medieval carpentry skill, in Jacobean stone masonry or the revolution in house plans were the product of such abilities – filtered down and emulated until original achievements became the norm.

There are two aspects to what is known as vernacular building. One is the use of local, indigenous materials as the mainstay – though there are exceptions. The pantiles of eastern coasts and river estuaries were originally imported from the Low Countries: the slates in many western areas came by sea from quarries far away, though on the same coastline. Nevertheless, the village brickworks, the local quarry, the stone from beach or field or hillside, were the supplies upon which the builder depended. The builder was also local; working for a lifetime within the immediate vicinity of his home. Nor were many of the builders more than odd-jobbers, in the modern sense. They probably combined a bit of small holding, another job or two and did building works when the season was right. Many small country builders, working on their own, still offer such a service.

One constant premise running through the gamut of traditional architecture is that the buildings should be functional, responding to their conditions and the use to which they are to be put. Simple practicality governed everything. In the farmstead, the requirements of animals and the storage and processing of crops, the tasks of the farmer and his wife were all linked. It still makes good sense to keep the animals close to their fodder; better still if that fodder can insulate their quarters too. With such simple considerations in mind, the effective machine of the pre-industrial farmyard developed. If that farm is in an area with a wet climate, the farmer's buildings must afford the maximum shelter to contents and to himself as he travels between them and, for the sake of their fabric, need to be protected as far as possible. No odd piece of slate or stone which protrudes inexplicably from a building is there to no purpose. Choice of site, the way in which materials were chosen and used, the form and disposition of buildings are all the result of long-held wisdom.

The end of the vernacular building era was not merely the curtailing of those links between a place and its buildings that once were taken for granted, but equally the rapid loss of that wisdom. Other factors now govern where a house is to be built, in what shape and plan and of what materials. The answers are not so different from one place to another and the builder has his basic range of skills – bricklaying, rough carpentry, and so on – but rarely the specific expertise which he needs to repair the traditional buildings of his area. Stone areas without competent stone masons, types of material which no one can repair because the techniques have been forgotten (earth building, in particular), old buildings ruined by crude work with rock-hard cement pointing or worms of raised mortar – all are the victims of this swift amnesiac reaction, effectively the process of the last fifty years.

In the television series which this book accompanies, we have tried to place the buildings of each region in the context both of their past, present and, sometimes, future. We want to show buildings in use as they had been designed – or as nearly as possible – and to offer some

Local limestone has furnished the building material here at Haunt Hill House, Great Weldon, Northamptonshire (above), including the transomed and mullioned window. A local family of masons, the Frisbeys, built this house for themselves.

The datestone over this window (right) is set into one of the ornamental lintels that decorate many doors and windows in the Lancashire Pennines.

explanations as to how that design had been arrived at. Why were some rooms in one place and not in another? Why does a timber-framed house have a brick or stone chimney? Hundreds of such questions have the simplest explanations; vernacular builders were never wilful or obscure. Their motives are there to be seen and understood. In domestic buildings, aspirations towards increasing comfort and space were important influences and the small touches of ornament, a fillip to the spirits, a bit of showing-off on the part of the craftsman, are part of that trend towards pleasurable as well as practical places. The chamfer on a fine piece of oak, the ornamental stone lintel with the date proudly inscribed, the pattern set into cobbles outside a front door are flourishes – the delight in the 'commodity firmness and delight' which have been upheld since antiquity as the components of fine architecture.

Each building, every area in this book and in the television series, tells us things. Within them you can read information – about people, history, economics and much more. They infer an inescapable continuity with a far from moribund past and offer lessons and pleasure in equal measure. Vernacular buildings are not the sentimental, picturesque backdrop to real life. They may be beautiful, but that is beside the point. They have emerged out of hard necessities, hard work and hard lives. Their appeal lies in the sense they make. The vernacular tradition is dead and it cannot be resurrected. It is for home truths, general principles and the indulgence of the eye that we value it. We are the fortunate heirs of this wealth.

Ornaments in stone, whether of lintels, gateposts or, as here, in the decorative patterning of the pathway to a front door, are a feature of the Bowland area of the Pennines. In Slaidburn such touches enliven the almost dour character of the cottages. This cottage is built of random stonework in which rough stones are all mortared into a whole.

Mid-Devon

The Coles family of Westacott have been working as thatchers since the 1700s.

The landscape of much of Devon, and in particular the broad central band between Dartmoor and Exmoor, has a comfortable feel about it. The low hills, upholstered with cushions of green or gold, red or brown, give an atmosphere rather like that of a well-furnished house. Everything is well ordered, from the intricate pattern of lanes – their widths still governed by pack-horse traffic rather than any wheeled vehicle – to the siting of the farms.

Celia Fiennes, travelling from Exeter to Chudleigh in 1698, described the scene much as it still is. She found 'mostly lanes and a continual going up hill and down, and all these lesser hills rises higher and higher till it advances you upon the high ridge, which discovers to view the great valleys below full of those lesser hills and inclosures, with quicksett hedges and trees, and rich land; but the roads are not to be seen, being all along in lanes ... on these hills one can discern little besides inclosures hedges and trees, rarely can see houses unless you are just descending to them, they allwayes are placed in holes as it were ...'

This area, which shares many characteristics with the east and south of the county, having the same geological characteristics based upon Old Red Sandstone, took on this pattern as it was developed by a numerous and highly prosperous race of Tudor yeoman farmers, in many respects the western counterpart of the Kentish yeoman.

This Farm in Black Torrington is ostensibly a seventeenth-century farmhouse, though evidence in its smoke-blackened roof proves it to be a medieval hall house, with two chimneys back to back and floors added at various times. Instead of the customary cross-passage, this house has a baffle entry.

The farmhouse and barns (right) near Woolfardisworthy are cob buildings which made use of a site providing the twin advantages of shelter and a south-facing position. A nearby spring is another good reason for the site.

Independent owner-occupiers, they combined a high degree of self-sufficiency with a well-developed mercantile skill. Thus their prosperity was largely based upon sheep – both for wool and meat. In the northern part, much of the meat trade was conducted with ships' victuallers. Cattle were kept too, for meat and for the family's needs. Arable crops were grown so that many of the holdings were mixed, but the smaller farms, on steep ground and poorer soil, confined themselves to supplying their own needs. The farmhouses of late medieval and Tudor date in this area offer the most solid proof of the wealth that these Devon yeoman farmers had amassed. They must provide as rich a selection of high-quality vernacular building as remains anywhere in Britain, vying with East Anglia, the Cotswolds and Kent, areas where wool was also the key to considerable widespread wealth.

In Devon these houses do not appear singly, but are dotted along the valleys which run through the area at frequent intervals. Little known rivers, such as the Creedy or the Troney, or better known ones, such as the Taw or the Yeo, are well endowed with countless such houses and even their insignificant tributaries, the little brooks which have carved out the lesser valleys of the area, can boast ancient farm sites on the hillsides above.

Many of these sites are commemorating much earlier farmsteads. The western extremities of Britain were settled early and remained stable: Bronze Age farmsteads set a precedent for the medieval and post-medieval farmers who merely sustained and developed what

The enclosed forecourt at Elston Barton, near Copplestone (left), has farm buildings making up the remaining three sides, a typical pattern in the larger farms in Devon. The barton is equivalent to the manor farm, and is likely to be the principal holding in the parish. Its design, largely confined to Devon, developed from the need to enclose the cattle. This house, cob and thatch, with mullioned windows, preserves a medieval screens passage so that the door here leads directly through to one on the opposite side. An oak post and panel screen marks this passage. The cobbles of the yard serve as a reminder that cobbled floors were also often found indoors.

Here at Stockland in east Devon (above) the use of cob died out early because of the sandstone which was found in the locality. Thatch remains the prevailing roofing material, however.

This corn barn (left) is built from the rich red earth of mid-Devon. The barn is linked to a series of enormous farm buildings, all of cob. Note the projecting midstrey.

This farm in Black Torrington (below) is thatched with Austrian water reed, a modern favourite because it comes from unpolluted waters. Typical of a house of medieval origin, it is carefully sited, dug back into the hillside. South-facing thatch lasts ten years longer than that facing the northerly direction.

had already become a way of life. The building of their fine farm-houses was approached with the usual expediency of country people. They had the raw materials to hand; the earth which furnished the cob walls, either a dun colour or an almost ruby red, and straw and timber to roof those walls over were available on every side. Straw and cob go together for another practical reason. Unbaked earth would not support the weight of a heavy roof clad in stone, tile or slate. Thatch was inevitably lighter. Even when walls have been ironed out and cement rendered, and roofs covered by slate or galvanised iron, the materials reveal themselves. Cob, which is a fine building material provided it is given 'a hat and a pair of shoes' – that is stone footings and deep eaves – and a render, traditionally lime-based, is a material which betrays its organic origins. There are no sharp corners in cob; walls seem to meander round to the back, and if a bread oven or staircase was required, a bulge was added to accommodate them. In this way the shape of the building seems merely to give a little, as required: a very different business to extending a building which was built in stone or brick when the need for courses and corners required a different kind of structural discipline altogether.

Similarly, the roofs stoop over the walls protectively and undulate along at eaves level. Many an iron roof, rusted to the tones of rich red cob, has been carefully cut into the line of dipping thatch eaves: some, of course, still cover the existing thatch which, on outbuildings in particular, proves prohibitively expensive to replace.

Cecil Torr in *Small Talk at Wreyland*, writing of life in the area in 1918, saw the beginning of the end for the widespread use of thatch. 'There is also a machine now to prepare wheat straw for thatching; and this bruises the reed, and renders it less durable than when it was prepared by hand. And now they never sow wheat early enough for the straw to gather strength. The result is that the thatch decays and landlords and farmers both get tired of patching it, and put up slate or iron instead, thereby helping to destroy the market for one of their own products.' He was not to know a time when farmers grew and harvested by binder special crops of wheat reed for thatching and could find it an immensely profitable enterprise. Thatch, now much in demand for domestic use, if not for the regular run of farm buildings as in the past, has made a turn round: combine harvesters and loss of local skills have helped to narrow the market and make both the materials and the skill itself sought after and well rewarded. Torr advances an eloquent justification for the use of thatch. 'Nobody,' he wrote, 'who has lived under a thatched roof would willingly live under any other – the comfort is so great. The thatch keeps out the cold in winter, and keeps out the heat in summer ... And really it is not inflammable. Just as paper will burn and books will not, so also straw will burn and and thatch will not: at least, thatch will only burn quite slowly like a book.'

A section of a kitchen garden wall of cob in Bow is here being rebuilt. The red clay and grit from the broken down section is reused, mixed with straw and some water. Previously oxen did the treading, and added their dung to the mixture, but now the treading is done by human feet (left). The cob is then slapped onto the wall on top of the vital stone footing which keeps the material dry. It is trodden down, working a section of 'lift' at a time (right). The wall will then be given a tiny roof to cap it and ensure the longevity of the cob – the best of all traditional materials.

Thatchers and thatch continue to meet demand. For cob, however, the position is dire. The thousands of cob buildings in Devon are disintegrating at an alarming rate: sometimes blockwork has been pieced in and the protection afforded by the roof pitch can ensure survival. But if the render has broken off, or as is frequently the case for farm buildings, the cob has remained unrendered, the material is vulnerable to wind and rain and Devon has plenty of both. Few people, even those in building, know the recipe for cob or have the desire to spend the necessary period stomping the clay, pebbles, straw and dung, which constitute the recipe, into the correct consistency. Cob can only be built in frost-free, dry weather, a small section at a time. The best that can be hoped for is that those cob buildings of special value will be repaired: the footings reinserted and heightened if necessary and the upper edge rebuilt in cob. There will be no new buildings in cob: Mr Alfred Howard's bus shelter at Down St Mary is the sole example. He has taken it upon himself, in his retirement, to pass on what he knows about the material so that a handful of local building workers will have the basic knowledge of the limits and possibilities of what was, until little more than a hundred years ago, Devon's principal building material, apart from the areas around Dartmoor, Exmoor and along parts of the southern coast where stone was more widely used. In mid-Devon, stone provided footings, chimney stacks and lintels.

Cecil Torr made his comments on cob too. 'Cob walls are as good as a thatched roof for resisting heat and cold; and the houses that have both, are far the best to live in, when the temperature out-doors is either high or low. The cob is made of clay and gravel kneaded together with straw, and is put up in a mass, like concrete. It is very durable, if kept dry . . . nine inches of brickwork, laid in cement, is as strong as eighteen inches of cob, and looks the same, if covered with cement and rough-cast. But the eighteen inches of cob keeps a house much warmer than eighteen of brick.' He goes on to talk about the use of local stone and, interestingly, about the prevalence of jerry-building, as much in the past as at the time of writing. The jerry-built structures of the past have fallen down. What remains is the best.

Timber, though seldom exposed on the outside, is one of the glories of the mid-Devon farmhouse. It is in the roof that the best clues to the age of a house lie: complex or rudimentary as the case may be, the joinery details sketch in the status of the early owner and the expertise of the carpenter. The cruck-framed roofs are commonly what is known as 'jointed cruck', that is made up with two sections of timber rather than a single rafter meeting its pair at the apex. The explanation is that the cruck is not fully load-bearing, and is therefore buried within the wall and needs to take far less weight. Exposed timber framing is not a Devon tradition and it is in the magnificent oak internal partitions or in the compartments of the finest ceilings, that the notable carpentry skills can be seen.

The jointed cruck was an expedient form of cruck framing when timber of a suitable length was scarce. Each cruck blade consists of two shaped timbers jointed together at the elbow.

Farmhouses in mid-Devon frequently point to thirteenth- or fourteenth-century pedigrees. These would have begun as hall houses, subdivided by head-height wooden partitions and with smoke from the centrally placed fire rising freely to the roof, though within the confines of a smoke bay, to blacken the underside of the rafters and thatch. A glimpse into the attic and other clues, such as the height of subsequent floors, can unravel the modifications and improvements that took place in many such houses – obviously their status being such that it was felt worthwhile to bring them into line with modern requirements rather than to demolish and start again.

A house such as Lower Chilverton, near Coldridge, shows its evolution clearly. Partial flooring over the open hall with chambers to each end was followed by a complete flooring-over in the seventeenth century, marked by the exceptional richness of the oak mouldings on the ceiling, and the insertion of a stone chimney stack to expel the smoke and provide a far more efficient source of heat. Here the main chimney was added to the side, or lateral wall of the house. Other examples had chimneys added axially. All these phases of alteration, which can be seen in the form of the building, are an illustration of more profound changes in the life, habits and expectations of the sixteenth- and seventeenth-century farmer. Privacy, a larger number of specifically functional rooms and an increasing wish for elegance and comfort can be seen emerging.

Jacobean ceiling, at
Westacott.

These diagrammatic
sections (opposite below)
show the evolution of a
yeoman farmhouse of
late medieval origin in
Devon. It was first an
open hall with a central
open hearth and low
partitions to divide off
the spaces of the house
(1). This was chambered
over either end, giving a
selection of rooms with
the heated, open hall
remaining (2). The last
stage, probably in the
late sixteenth century,
was the contruction of a
solid masonry chimney
stack and the addition of
a ceiling to the hall (3).

The cross-passage was a constant feature in these houses. Comparable to the division between the quarters for the humans and the animals in the longhouse, found on the fringes of Dartmoor and occasionally elsewhere in Devon, the division in the larger farmhouse was between three rooms, all for the use of the farmer and his family. Two rooms, both warmed by the hearth, were living quarters, the third on the so-called lower side of the passage, was for servicing the household, that is for preparing or storing food. At Prowse, a farmhouse near Sandford, the cross-passage is paved with cobbles and is abnormally wide suggesting that it might have been designed for the passage of laden animals rather than for the people of the house to go from one part to another. The usual flooring for a cross-passage is flagstone and the post and panel oak screen that often forms one side of the passage (hence 'screens passage') is sometimes elaborated or even painted with the door marked out by details such as shoulders with chamfering. Hill at Christow is a house which has both an intact flagged screens passage and, in this scale of house, an extremely rare open hall which has never been roofed over.

It also demonstrates another feature common in yeoman farmhouses here – an elaborate plaster ceiling. The largest houses, the manors or bartons, had possibly set the fashion and had encouraged a local expertise, but the smaller houses have many comparable examples. One version of events is that these ceilings were a traditional wedding gift, certainly they are often placed in the upper chamber, although many houses have one on each floor. Jacobean in their elaborate strapwork and formalised flower patterns, they are one of the glories of these houses.

Unusually, this area has seen a complete turn-round in ownership and the farms that were built by independent owner-occupiers in the Tudor period have, more often than not, passed into the hands of large estates, only to be sold back as family farms this century. The burden of maintenance then falls on the farmer's shoulders and despite a helpful county council and the availability of grants, the sums involved in such repairs can be awe-inspiring.

Many farmhouses have a sizeable dairy, either within the house itself or immediately adjacent. Mid-Devon was not a great cheese-producing area like Somerset but in the era before centralised milk collection and sales (begun in the late 1930s) surplus milk was used in the most practical way possible. Clotted, or scalded, cream was one local speciality. Similarly the production of cider was widespread, but generally for the consumption of family or neighbours. That process merited a purpose-built structure, the pound house, in which, from the late seventeenth century, a donkey would propel the grinding apparatus which converts the apples to liquid.

The other specifically local building type is the linhay, or linney, which takes into account the climatic factors and turns them to advantage in the time-honoured fashion of the vernacular builder.

This farmhouse (above) is at Westacott, near Bow. Beneath its cob and thatch there is evidence of a medieval hall house. The obvious signs of its earlier affluence are, however, to be found in a sixteenth-century addition. This is the cross wing with a ten-light window demarcated by splendid oak 'king'

mullions (right) and inside, two elaborate Jacobean plaster ceilings, one upstairs and one down (opposite left). A great pit nearby shows the source of the cob for the house and the sizeable barns that surround it.

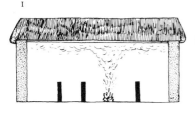

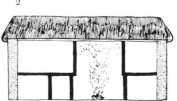

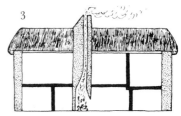

A farmhouse near Crediton (right) shows the customary careful siting; it is both sheltered and far enough above the valley bottom to avoid the mist and damp. A water source will have determined the actual spot.

A linhay (below) is a specifically Devon type of farm building, with its enclosed cattle stalls below and the open-fronted hay loft (tallet). This one is at Lower Chilverton Farm, Coldridge.

With a damp climate, the hay is stored in an open-fronted, upper-level loft or tallet – open in order that wind and sun can dry it, but facing away from the prevailing south-westerly winds so that rain-water cannot be driven in. Below, cattle are housed over-winter in the shippon; warmed and fed from above (as in the Pennine barn-cum-shippon), but again well aired by an often partially open-fronted arrangement. The supports for the tallet are of timber, stone or, less often, brick. Cob was less suited here but provides the deep back and side walls, except for the one which catches the prevailing wind built more usually in stone.

The siting and positioning of buildings was an art based on considerable native cunning. As Celia Fiennes noted they are often well down into the valley, but equally they are rarely actually at the bottom, where risk of flooding and the frequent possibility of low-lying mists made that an unattractive prospect. Just as in Wales, the site chosen was usually about a third of the way up the valley, probably near a spring, with maximum shelter from wind and maximum exposure to the sun. Often a nearby pond shows the exact source of the cob. The site was a marvellous product of foresight, experience and common sense and Professor Hoskins has found that the best sites are, perhaps inevitably, the earliest.

The materials were handled to suit their position. If the back of the house was buried in the hillside, the stone footings were carried up, well above the ground, to avoid damp penetrating the vulnerable cob. Rough-cast render was generally applied, at least on the exposed elevations of the house, and then lime-washed over, and often the side facing south west was built entirely of stone. Floors in the early houses, and certainly in the humbler cottages, were of ash and lime, which when stamped down hard with a heavy clay layer beneath was impermeable. Sometimes it was polished up with soot.

The barns on these Devon farmsteads, although usually much later in date than the houses, conform to the pattern of all mixed farms with a bias toward pastoral agriculture. They are smaller than their counterparts in eastern or midland Britain, but still preserve the essentials – the threshing floor (in the nineteenth century, sometimes with a round house appended) and the separate storage areas for straw and grain. In Devon the storage of wool or grain was usually in an upper room of an outbuilding or in the attics of the house. The same factors of security and dryness governed the storage of these valuable commodities as when the purpose-built granary was provided. Many barns in Devon are cruck framed – usually home-spun versions of the cruck frames buried beneath many of the hall houses. There are surprises here and there. At Prowse, the wing which lies at right-angles to the main house has magnificent wind-braced timbers and shouldered doors which would imply origins as a particularly grand room; now, its state of preservation is due to long years of use as a barn.

Mid-Devon is characterised by a regular smattering of farmsteads, by a number of prosperous small market towns and also by a distinct category of settlement – those many villages which tried to obtain status as towns, gained it and then reverted to villages once more, still bearing the pattern and architecture of a more substantial place. There are many to cite, but Witheridge is a good example. It has a bewildering great market square with solid cob and thatch houses surrounding it and forming narrow closes and alleys off, and yet nothing much beyond that. It achieved its charter as a market town in 1248 and has functioned ever since as a local centre, albeit one which serves a relatively small locality.

Apart from variations in the tones that exhibit the local choice of materials, such as the earth, veering from the plum-red of the band which stretches west beyond Crediton to the duller, mousey browns of the soil in the rest of the region, and the same variation between the grey of granite and the dark ochre of the sandstone in the footings and chimney stacks, mid-Devon is remarkably homogenous in its buildings.

Henry James, an American visitor to Devon in the late nineteenth century, described the scene thus: 'A Devonshire cottage is no less striking an outcome of the ages and the seasons and the manners.

Crushed beneath its burden of thatch, coated with a rough white stucco of a tone to delight a painter, nestling in deep foliage and garnished at doorstep and wayside with various forms of chubby infancy, it seems to have been stationed there for no more obvious purpose than to keep a promise to your fancy, though it covers, I suppose, not a little of the sordid side of life which the fancy likes to slur over.'

Witheridge, with its large marketplace now surplus to requirements, is a reminder that many Devon villages were ambitious to become trading centres and few succeeded. Here houses of cob and thatch were superseded in the nineteenth century by those built of brick and slate.

The breadth of Devon's past prosperity is measured in the spread of sophisticated houses which fall into that ill-defined category of traditional or vernacular architecture. The development of these buildings might echo patterns handed down from the great houses, but they are introduced in a fresh way, in the manner of this particular area. Just as the robust, closely packed timbers of the Wealden house has come to represent the yeoman farmer of that corner of England so, too, the organic forms of the hunched Devon farmhouse and its encircling farm buildings conjure up the preferences of generations of Tudor farmers, discovering and building upon the idea of home comfort as well as creating functional and appealing places.

The Weald

A good example of a
Wealden house is this
one at Headcorn. (The
word weald in old
English meant forest.)

The wealth of the Wealden landscape is illustrated almost ostentatiously in its vegetation, its agriculture, its building materials and the architecture that has evolved from that. The clue lies in the rich, clay soil that makes up the Weald, through Kent and Sussex into Surrey, and the beneficiaries have been the small-scale, independent farmers whose thickly hedged pastures shelter the cattle and sheep.

It has long been a trim, orderly scene with orchards and hop gardens providing interludes between the fields and coppiced woodland. Celia Fiennes described it in 1697, looking down from a 'very high hill' (presumably the North Downs) between Maidstone and Canterbury: it 'commands the view of the Country a vast way, and with such a variety of woods rivers and inclosures and buildings that was very delicate and diverting'. It is that combination of a tightly reined-in nature and a sympathetic architecture that still marks the views from the North Downs (as for example near Egerton) over the Weald beyond Tunbridge Wells. The buildings are, in the affluence of fine carpentry, confident brickwork and tile-hanging, of a piece. They share in the good oak and heavy clay of the landscape.

It is a warm scene. Burnt sienna tiles on roofs or walls, brick echoing the same tones; no-nonsense black or white weather-boarding provides the sharp notes; even the greyest days are less chill with this palette. In winter the hop gardens are bare of all foliage. In summer and spring they are jungles, verdant and dense until stripped away in October. Four-square orchards, aisled like the hop gardens, are echoed in the domestic containment of the rectangular Wealden farmhouse, enveloped comfortably under a tea-cosy of a roof.

It is the unremitting bleakness of the Romney Marsh that under-pins the economy of the Weald. In those stark expanses, prised back from the sea over the centuries, the sheep and cattle, which end their days fat in the little Wealden pastures, are grazed on some of the best land in the country. The Wealden grazier and his marshland counter-part have always been interconnected, sometimes one man farms land in both areas, but his house is generally safely above water level, on the old cliffs that separate the two. The grazier-butcher combined both rôles and the numerous butchers' shops remaining in the Kent and Sussex villages are reminders of that, although modern hygiene regulations make this combination impossible.

The yeoman farmer, owner and cultivator of his own land, deter-mined the pattern of settlement in the Weald from the late medieval period as the woodland was pushed aside to increase the area of grazing land. Until then, the density of the forest and the heaviness of the clay had deterred development and there had been insufficient demand for land to make clearance a matter of any urgency. Agri-culture made the first inroads, iron smelting – based on available ore and charcoal – the next. It was the farmers, the iron masters and the wool merchants who made up the prosperous class who, from the fifteenth century on, were to build a succession of finely constructed houses of a type which would have been inconceivable at the time in the more culturally remote areas of the country.

The oaks which thrived on the clay of the Weald, and whose timbers furnished the coastal ship-building industry, were the stuff of these houses. A particular model of a late medieval hall house is now known as the 'Wealden house' which, although it does appear else-where in England, is found in unprecedented numbers in the Weald even today. There were different types based on the pattern but these only constituted variations of an enduring theme which remained constant until the mid-sixteenth century. Originally centred on the core of an open hall, displaying a fine crown post as a structural pin as much as a decorative flourish, the Wealden house proper is typified by a central recessed bay and a slight outward projection, known as a jetty, of the two flanking bays at first-floor height. Another varia-tion, widely found throughout the same belt, has a jettied upper storey projecting on one or both of the end walls, rather than on the front elevation. In addition to the oak of the main constructional members, the houses are infilled by wattle and daub panels plastered over, and have deep-hipped or half-hipped roofs covered by densely packed small plain tiles.

Agricultural or industrial wealth provided the Wealden carpenters with ample opportunity to practise and refine their considerable skills. The complex roof structures, with the crown post as eye-catcher, the detail of the chamfered mullions and the fine tongue-and-groove doors, together with the sure touch with which the wall and roof timbers were jointed and pegged into place, attest to a large band of highly skilled carpenters working both in town and village and out in the open countryside. As the domestic arrangements of the yeoman farmer became more elaborate, and his house, by the Tudor period, had become furnished with a wide range of articles, so the open hall was floored over and the house further subdivided. Inevitably a substantial brick chimney was inserted and sometimes the interstices between the wall posts were filled by brick in preference to the flimsier wattle and daub or its later replacement, lathe and plaster. The sophistication of these houses and their ready adaptability in the hands of later generations has been their best defence against redundancy and demolition: some ostensibly late seventeenth- or early eighteenth-century houses in the area are, on closer examination, mere masks to earlier Wealden houses, refronted or perhaps extended around the original core. As a type of house which has remained appropriate in scale, appealing to the eye and adaptable in its internal arrangements, it has few peers. Generations of farmers have found them adequate and now their attraction is seen in vastly inflated property prices, ensuring that the only new owners of a late medieval Wealden house are the very wealthy.

For the Victorians, in particular a whole generation of artists, the yeoman farmhouse and even the humbler tile-hung Wealden cottage were perfect examples of a picturesque rural architecture and they were used, by implication at least, as images of rustic continuity, a bulwark against the spectre of industrialisation. As the farmer's house was idealised into a pictorial or verbal image, so the man himself was represented as a personification of similar solid values and virtues, based upon his independence and hence his freedom from the taint of the modern world. The yeoman farmer was an appealing image in political terms too; at one extreme far from the taint of either feudalism or paternalism, on the other far removed from collectivism.

When George Meredith wrote *Diana of the Crossways* there was no yeoman farmer in the picture, but the image of the house, transposed from its real site in Abinger, Surrey into Sussex, is a powerful one. As in the book, it remains a romantic house, built in the early seventeenth century of brick, sandstone and a Horsham slate roof. It has an enclosed garden forecourt and a storeyed-over porch, while its windows are generous, lighting low-ceilinged rooms, all pivoted around a splendid central stair with carefully carved bannisters and newels. The timber-framed Wealden house and its later counterpart, the brick farmhouse of the seventeenth and eighteenth centuries, are among the most evocative of the traditional buildings to be found anywhere and they cannot fail to recapture the lives and the domestic values which guided their builders and occupants.

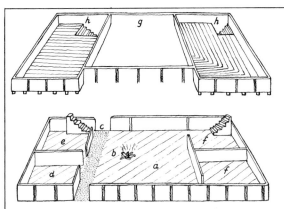

a) hall b) open hearth c) cross passage d) buttery e) pantry f) unheated parlours g) full height hall h) chambers
The plan of the Wealden house shows the two floors with the service areas and parlours beneath and the chambers above. The house is characterised by jettied chambers at one or both ends. A Wealden house at Headcorn (right and below) has a double-height window which marks the centre recessed bay. This was full height, in contrast to the jettied chambers at either end.

If the Wealden landscape and its occupants have tended to provide idealised images to support abstract notions, the realities are harsher. This part of south-eastern England has an exposed climate, with blistering easterly winds and notorious frosts; it is no accident that the frequent addition to village names 'Forstal' is in fact a contraction of 'frost hollow'. The buildings too, despite their reassuring solidity and pleasing materials, are to considerable measure merely the expression of the conditions. By the early eighteenth century, the best oak had been felled and smaller houses and cottages were often less well built, using inferior timber and flimsy panels of infill or poor brickwork. Thus the cladding of weather-boarding, lapped softwood timber, or the use of vertical tiles was primarily practical, weather-proofing skin over the inferior layer below. The idea of using the tiles decoratively by alternating rows of fish-tail or club-shaped tiles with the standard scale or plain tile, came later, making the best of the job.

Apart from the timber-framed yeoman farmhouses and later brick-built houses, which took on the classical formality and detail of larger, architect-designed houses of the late seventeenth and eighteenth century, there is a range of purpose-built agricultural buildings which are equally characteristic of the Weald, using local materials to functional ends. Although the agricultural balance was always in favour of a pastoral economy, in the past a certain amount of arable land was maintained to provide fodder for the animals and for extra income and domestic supplies. Small granaries on staddle stones, or piers, walled in weather-boarding, brick and timber or tile-hung, were one structure developed to house grain. They are rarely earlier than the eighteenth century since before that grain was generally housed at the top of the farmhouse. The interiors were divided into a series of wooden bins and the entire area was carefully designed to be both secure and dry. The staddle stones deterred theft by vermin, and strong doors and windows kept out human thieves. They were lined with boarding and covered with plaster as extra protection.

Although in parts of the south east, east of Canterbury for example, where arable farming was on a large scale, vast tithe barns were to be found, in the Weald the needs were simpler. A farmer required storage for hay or straw and quite possibly winter accommodation for his cattle: both could be provided under the same roof, and the building was usually a timber-framed one, with weather-board cladding, which varied little in type from the seventeenth to the nineteenth centuries, though its pattern was established earlier still. Tarred black, with warm, red-tiled roofs, there are hundreds of such barns in both the Kent and Sussex Weald, sometimes huddled close to the farmhouse, sometimes out in the fields nearer to crops and cattle. It is not easy to guess the date of such buildings for the cladding might hide a skeleton of perhaps Tudor date, and only minor variations will give some clue to an experienced eye as to its history.

This weather-board granary, timber-framed and clad in lapped softwood, rests on staddle stones. These mushroom-shaped stones deterred rats and mice from climbing into the building and consuming the valuable grain. The secure door and upper access to a further loft are the sole means in or out of this purpose-built grain bin.

36

A cottage in the Weald (left) in which timber framing can be seen at ground level with weather-board cladding above it.

The white cowls of a pair of oasts (below) peep out from the trees in the Kentish Weald. The cowls provided the draught for the kiln below and are now redundant since a modern kiln is no longer fired by charcoal.

These cottages at Smarden provide a characteristic mixture of Wealden materials – tiles and weather-boarding. This was proof against a tough winter climate and an extra skin over inferior materials.

Crossways Farm, Abinger Hammer, inspired George Meredith in his novel _Diana of the Crossways_. A mixture of sandstone from a quarry in the valley, decorative brickwork, tile hanging and Horsham slates (on the roof), it is the perfect embodiment of a yeoman's farmhouse of the first half of the seventeenth century. The gabled entrance porch and the great chimney stacks are notable features of a house which celebrates the new domestic comforts of the period.

While the cattle could be housed snugly with their winter fodder, sheep required no specialised buildings. Nor did another staple crop of the Kentish Weald, fruit: hops, on the other hand, did. Kentish hop gardens have a lengthy history. They date from at least the sixteenth century when Protestant refugees came to this part of the country which offered suitable soil and climate, a good supply of wood (sweet chestnut) for poles, and a ready labour force. Kilns were necessary and it soon became essential to design a specialised structure for this purpose. Rectangular drying houses were suggested by one authority as early as 1574 and it was this shape that the early oasts followed. To ensure a good strong draught over the burning coal or charcoal, the characteristic cowl appeared and this was usually designed in conjunction with a circular oasthouse: until the late nineteenth century this became the usual form, and then the oast returned to a square shape, easier to build and just as effective.

The oast house is the perfect example of a building designed on purely functional lines. It was changed only in order to facilitate the process: if something seemed to work better in another shape, or in another position, then the building was altered accordingly. The oast house developed in response to these needs alone. A vertical arrangement seemed to be the best internal plan: the hops were brought, green, onto the outside platform, then shovelled onto sacking to dry over the heat, put into a cooling space alongside, and then packed, by stamping down, into the 'pockets' – the long, thin, sacks in which hops are still put – which were then dropped down to ground level for transport to the brewery. A town such as Faversham is still strongly tied economically to the hop, even if the product which reaches the breweries is now a processed pellet bearing no resemblance to the original husk.

Now that functioning oast houses do not need the cowl because they are fired by gas, oil or electricity, the form of the building no longer makes sense in its traditional shape. A modern kiln can be housed anywhere, in any kind of purpose-built shed or existing structure. Most eighteenth- or nineteenth-century oasts which are still in use have been extended. Only one oast house in the Weald, near Smarden, uses the coal-fired system and requires its cowl.

As a feature within the landscape, the white capped oast, or group of oasts, looking like packs of beer cans tightly bundled into twos or fours, is most people's image of the Kentish Weald. Cresting the waves of trees, they are the dominant feature in the panorama of the Weald that can be glimpsed from higher ground, here and there. Yet almost all of these buildings are now out of use, redundant and empty if farmers have resisted the pressure and financial inducements of selling the buildings off – usually for conversion into awkwardly domesticised houses. Often they are travestied, with casement windows and all manner of extraneous features removing the basic appeal, the simplicity of form and the directness of purpose.

The oast house (right) is a circular brickwork structure with a weather-boarded drying chamber in front. These pictures show the hops coming in from a hop garden at Smarden by tractor (above). They are then bagged and put on the platform (left) before being taken into the kiln for drying.

The siting of the farms and farm buildings in the Weald reflects the nature of the land ownership: this is not an area of estates, nor was it formerly one of open-field farming, with the farmers congregated in the villages and cultivating land scattered widely outside. It is the province of the owner-occupier, who built his house and outbuildings in the midst of his fields, giving the countryside a built-up appearance far removed from the great expanses of farmland in the Midlands or East Anglia. Hardly a view across the Weald does not, as Celia Fiennes commented three hundred years ago, reveal a patchwork made up in equal measure of woodland, hedges, pasture and buildings. It makes an harmonious whole. In the villages and highly prosperous small market towns of the Weald the houses are those of the merchants who sold or processed agricultural goods or those of the iron industry. Alongside these are terraced or double cottages, mostly of eighteenth- or nineteenth-century date, built of brick and tile or weather-board, which give these places, whether lined up along the high street or around the churchyard or village green, a substantial, almost urban air. Smarden, Biddenden, Tenterden in the Kentish Weald or Wadhurst in Sussex all have this air of all's well with the world sustained by their availability for commuters to London and their appeal to a wealthy retired population.

This plain tile-hung cottage is at Witley in Surrey. The use of clay tiles hung vertically is a characteristic of the Weald where suitable clay is readily found. The tiles serve to weatherproof less substantially built cottages.

An alternative to tile
hanging was the use of
lapped softwood as an
extra skin on a house.
This weather-board
house is at Smarden
(right). The practice is
common in the south-
eastern counties of
England.

The main street in
Smarden (below) shows
the way in which
cottages and houses have
filled up to form a
continuous road
frontage.

The Weald of Kent and Sussex grew rich on wool. The sheep were grazed on the nearby Romney Marsh and the traditional shepherd of the area, the 'looker', spent his time in this hut. The chimney denotes a fireplace which gave the looker, and any ailing lambs in his charge, warmth.

Down on the marshes, the older buildings are concentrated on higher ground, above the waterlogged, reclaimed Romney Marsh, which achieved its present form by the mid-seventeenth century. More recently, with more secure drainage, the villages have spread and some farms stand out in the open, marking the position of the roads. Most characteristic of the buildings in this area, however, have been the lookers' huts – now redundant and fast disappearing. Here, that specifically marshland race, the lookers or self-employed shepherds, would spend weeks at a time with their sheep. The hut, a tiny brick box with a chimney, was home during the lambing season or while the flock grazed at distant pasture.

Apart from the Wealden oak, it is still the Wealden clay that determines the architectural style of the area. The numerous ponds sited close to farmhouses attest to clay being dug on the spot to provide the materials for the house. Local brick and tile works supplied the hand-made materials which, until industrialisation in the mid-nineteenth century, supplied bricks and tiles with the variation in tone and finish that marks out the hand-made article from the standardised and homogenous product of a mechanised process. Within the area there are still a handful of businesses following the old lines. It is ironic that, with the renewed interest in traditional materials – both for repair of old buildings and in some cases for the finishing touches to new ones – the demand for such bricks and tiles has grown enormously in the last few years. The taste for bland, often garish, brick has palled and the flawed and textured surfaces of the hand-made article seem ever more appealing by comparison.

Yet a return to traditional materials, a taste for historic houses and an apparently unchanging form of agriculture disguise enormous change in this area. The proximity to London, the expansion of towns such as Maidstone or Ashford, the ever-widening commuter belt stretching through the three counties have distorted the values of the existing houses whilst virtually freezing any new development. However, here as elsewhere farm amalgamation, pressure to enlarge field size and alter the type of cultivation have had their effect. The loss of small oasts is an example of these pressures: hop gardens grow larger and less numerous in deference to the brewers' demands.

Few farmhouses house farmers: even fewer oasts still house hop-drying kilns. The Weald is, in some areas, little more than a skin of historic buildings and a landscape which remains intact, stretched across the face of a dramatically altered rural area. It is the buildings that help preserve the illusion of no change: it is, in some ways, their very appeal that has brought about those changes from the moment when, in the nineteenth century, the artists, writers and literati of London started to move out to the peaceful villages of Kent, Sussex and Surrey. Witley, Penshurst and many more saw their first urban refugees in the 1860s. They have never been able to shake them off. It was a crumbling Wealden house, the Clergy House at Alfriston in Sussex, which brought about the foundation of the National Trust. So the Weald has become the image of rural stability for the highly urbanised south east of England.

These terraced cottages of brick with their tiled roofs and gabled porches are in the village of Witley.

Suffolk and Essex

Lavenham has many perfect examples of fifteenth-century hall houses; this one is the Old Wool Hall, which remains open to the rafters.

There was little choice in the matter of building materials for the Tudor farmer or the seventeenth-century labourer in much of East Anglia. Unlike many other areas in which builders used timber and mud for construction until stone pre-empted them, there is no good building stone here. There is a handful of materials (with considerable deficiencies, it is true) and the doughty East Anglians tried them all. There was chalk and flint and even a curious conglomerate stone known as septaria which appeared, exposed, along the coast and estuaries in northern Essex and Suffolk. The latter was seized upon by the Romans and appeared in various castles and churches in the area until the mid-sixteenth century. Septaria, a young, scarcely solidified stone, chalk, a friable material which has to be worked with great care and expertise, and flint, an obdurate and impervious stone, are a triumvirate of almost impossible building materials. No wonder that the art of carpentry, as exemplified in the timber-framed buildings of this region, flourished unchallenged until the art of the bricklayer superseded it from the seventeenth century onwards.

Boulder clay is the geologically dominant feature of this region: it has determined the landscape, buildings and agricultural practice of almost all of Essex, all but the north west of Suffolk and most of east Norfolk. Here and there chalk land bleaches the tones and enlarges the scale to the extremities of vision with unbroken downland. It was,

49

however, the clay that nurtured the oaks which gave the medieval carpenter his raw material.

High-quality hardwood, providing that most durable of materials, the heart of oak, and good clay were the basis of the traditional buildings in East Anglia. Nothing much went to waste. Straw doubled for thatch and as a binding agent worked into the clay, with manure, to make daub or clay bat walling, while along the river estuaries water reeds provided roofing and flooring material. Later, the clay was fired in kilns, which stood in almost every village, and this provided bricks and tiles of many different shades and shapes. When good timber became scarce, inferior hard or softwoods from the locality or imported from Scandinavian neighbours, were pressed into service as weather-board cladding for less important buildings, the barns and other functional structures of the countryside such as wind and watermills. That pattern is one of the many legacies which this region bequeathed to the eastern seaboard of the United States where clapboard is the true vernacular material over a vast area.

The buildings of north Essex and Suffolk seem to express their origins in the ground by their very forms: soft corners, the sign of clay walling, the bulging thatch and the gentle irregularities of timber framing are all far from the precise lines of coursed machine brick or even the measured pattern of ashlared blocks of stone. The organic forms of traditional construction seem almost to have been picked up in the language – vernacular terms such as clunch (for chalk blocks) or clay bat have a solid ring to them.

A detail of the Old Wool Hall in which close studding, strengthened by wind braces, with jetties and oak mullioned windows are all typical of East Anglian timber-framed construction.

The landscape and the traditionally constructed buildings fit together effortlessly. The rounded thatched shoulders of cottage and barn emerge over the gently undulating land. Punctuating the horizon more stridently are the tall brick chimney stacks of the large farmhouses, sometimes elaborated into twisting corkscrews of small Tudor bricks, while the village church towers (rarely spires) seem to congregate, five or six at a glance, in almost every direction you care to look. Recent eradication of hedges and woodland make these accents even more prominent.

Although carbon-dating has identified the timbers in a couple of timber-framed buildings in Essex as being of the eleventh century, it was from the thirteenth century onwards that the carpentry skills began to be developed which would give these counties, with Kent, Sussex and Surrey, their pre-eminence in the system known as box-frame construction. At first these skills were developed in the service of wealthy churchmen and landowners but over the centuries these builders served the needs of a much wider section of society. Any farmer who could afford the labour and materials and any merchant who could find a plot of town land was to benefit. The towns and villages, as well as the outlying farms of a rich yeoman class, were being built on the proceeds of the wool trade, just as in the stone areas of the Cotswolds and further east into Northampton and the east Midlands, people were building on the profits of their sheep. Weavers' cottages are another widespread feature of the landscape serving to remind us of the importance of wool in the East Anglian economy.

In contrast to the western and north-western parts of the country where the A-formed cruck was the prevailing timber-framing pattern, in this area and in the adjacent counties of Cambridgeshire, Hertfordshire and Bedfordshire in particular, the system was that of a balloon frame, in which the walls were lightly pinioned by the roof timbers. The thrusts and counterthrusts of the whole were finely balanced and contained by an intricate system of joints of various kinds: comparable in importance to the role played by the joints in the human frame. Externally the walls were of vertical timbers (known as close-studding because they were usually set densely) only broken by the principal horizontal beam demarcating floor levels. Thus the form of the interior of the house can be read from the outside, unlike the bland surface offered by a masonry structure. This method of framing required large quantities of high-quality oak which points to the considerable wealth and established economic status of the men who built houses on these lines. The other ostentatious sign is the crown post, the pivotal structural element in the roof assembly, which in better quality houses was decorated. After the early sixteenth century, the crown post gave way to a variety of alternative roof frames and so the crown post helps to date the house.

The timber-framed house was quite a flexible affair. It allowed for building on, either in the form of a cross wing, or by dropping the

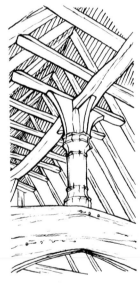

An ornamental crown post with its embellished capital supports a collar purlin (the longitudinal beam) upon which rest collars. These collars join the rafters which cross the open hall. In less important buildings, the crown post would be left plain.

A corner of the Old Wool Hall (near right) shows the careful ornamentation. The carved capital on the corner post and the detail on the bressumer mark this building out as an important structure on which exceptional skills were employed. Notice the brackets which support the jetty. The timber frame has a brick footing which protects the sill from damp.

The Little Hall, Lavenham (far right), is now the home of the Suffolk Preservation Society and is open to the public. It is a fifteenth-century hall house with double-height windows. The timber has been lime-washed in the traditional fashion as a method of protection.

The Barley and Wheat barns (left and right in the picture) are at Cressing Temple in Essex. Although they have been substantially rebuilt on the outside, the interior timber framing of the two buildings has been carbon-dated to, respectively, the first and second halves of the thirteenth century.

roof almost to ground level as an outshot, which was generally sited to the north of the house providing a cool spot for the service rooms. Jetties – overhanging upper storeys – were a feature of town houses and later of country ones. Their precise significance seems to have puzzled all the experts, but they did allow for extra space at the upper level, even if that gain was minimal. Like close studding, the jetty appears to have been something of a status symbol.

Another system of timber framing to be found widely in the area also offers more space internally; this is the aisled building in which additional posts, the arcade posts, demarcate a 'nave' allowing a system of roof trusses to encompass a wider area, including two side aisles. Despite the obstruction offered by the posts, which tends to make it a less practical plan for domestic purposes, the aisled frame was widely chosen for barns since the subsidiary space could be used for storage, or other functions not directly associated with the threshing barn, such as housing cattle.

The threshing barns of Essex and Suffolk repeat the established format of such buildings across the arable land of Britain. At its simplest, the plan is based upon three bays, two of them flanking the central threshing bay. Entry is often beneath a canopied porch, the midstrey, and the threshing floor lies transverse with the opposing doors designed to give the maximum through draught. In Essex and Suffolk these barns are often weather-boarded and tarred for preservation. Threshed and unthreshed straw was stored in the two adjacent bays; grain was stored elsewhere, in the house, over a cartshed or, less often here, in a purpose-built granary.

Agricultural buildings might be built of best oak to ensure their longevity (an investment which has proved entirely justifiable, considering that some of the great corn barns have stood for five or even six hundred years), but domestic buildings justified more attention to detail. One of the attractions of the timber-framed buildings of the region are the flourishes – the hidden piece of elegant carpentry which is the personal touch of the man who left it there. This is the expression of pleasure in a job well done, the kind of satisfaction that can be picked up in conversation with his descendants, the builders who work on the repair of traditional architecture. Sometimes the work of maintaining the medieval or Tudor buildings requires a care and skill commensurate with the standards of the original work. To dovetail a piece of new oak into the old joint, or to pin a worn timber back on to the repaired framework is to experience satisfaction in the work of your hands, as well as the emotion of making contact with the craftsmen of the past. The creative and the functional approaches are so closely integrated that they are hardly divisable.

Fashion touched details cursorily. Castellated decoration along the bressumer beam is one which reflects the attention paid in the fifteenth century to the Gothic style and clues can be gained from the carved capital upon a corner post or the ornamental flourishes over

Falconer's Hall, Good Easter, Essex, is an aisled corn barn, still in agricultural use, which contains the principal posts of the late eleventh-century prebendal hall. Extended and remodelled at a much later date, the proof of the antiquity of the posts (foreground left and right) is the way in which they were shored from underground and the pattern of the Norman cushion capitals.

a door or window. A particular carpenter might favour a small variation on a standard joint and the formulation of a system of roof trusses would change as better ideas suggested themselves in the light of long experience. However, generally little changed. Although the timber-framed buildings still standing are apparently but a fraction of those that once made up the built landscape of town, village and countryside of eastern England, this number is an impressive tribute to the quality of both materials and methods of construction. That quality has willed longevity on these buildings, as on those of Kent or along the Welsh borders which share a distinct pattern of timber framing and the same extraordinarily resilient timber. They remain almost indestructible until the loss of a roof following long dereliction sounds the death-knell.

Nowadays, a timber-framed house is a marketable proposition to the extent that modern timber-framed houses, attempting to replicate traditional joinery skills, are being sold at inflated prices to an eager market. The originals have often suffered a fate worse than destruction, with the taste for 'Tudorisation' that makes the ancient timber look new, the crooked walls straight and goes to town on so-called period detail. One misplaced modern enthusiasm is for stripping away the plaster to expose beams which generally were meant to be hidden. The principal beams, as can be seen from their detail or ornamentation, were designed to be exposed; the remainder, hatched for the daub or plaster to find a hold, was to remain unseen. Similarly the dark staining instigated in the Victorian period to emphasise the black and white effect is incorrect. A coat of lime wash, lightening the tone of the oak, is the best protection and the traditional one.

Between the timber studs, the panels of these houses were constructed of a mesh of wattle and daub and later lath and plaster. At a time when brick was becoming a status symbol of the sixteenth-century building world, it was also used in the interstices of the timber framing, set in a cunning herring-bone pattern which was known as nogging.

The plaster coating, coloured with tinted lime wash, was put to good use on these buildings, encouraging the specifically local skill of pargetting. In Norfolk the same practice was named 'pinking' so that pargetting is properly the hallmark of the areas of Suffolk and Essex with which this chapter is concerned. In the small towns and villages along the Stour Valley, such as Boxford, Stoke-by-Nayland or Bures, innumerable variations upon this theme can be seen.

There were two types of work: impressed geometric patterns or more elaborate raised relief work, made elsewhere and then bonded onto the plasterwork. The former consisted of a limited repertoire of patterns, pressed into wet lime plaster with a wooden stamp (later, an iron one). It was the essentially soft lines of the plaster that established the character of the pargetting: modern work tends to be

Traditional Suffolk pink colour wash covers this thatched cottage in Lindsey (top left).

The Grange at Chelsworth, Suffolk, has its date of 1694 over the door (top right). The house is probably earlier and the door and cartouche merely final flourishes at the end of the building programme.

This large Tudor farmhouse (below right) is sited well out in the countryside away from the village of Preston, Suffolk. This reflects the status of the independent farmer of Tudor times who farmed his own acreage.

This thatched cottage is sited just outside the village of Great Dunmow in Essex. A pond in a village such as this served to water stock on their way to market.

The large pond in front of this farmhouse (left) near Edwardstone in Suffolk probably commemorates an earlier moat. The yeoman farmhouse is typical of the late Tudor period.

marred by the hard nature of a cement-based mix. In fact, pargetting, so labour intensive and time consuming, is, in its traditional form, almost dead. Demand is now for more fanciful motifs, perhaps a play upon the name of the householder or house, and often far from the spirit of simple ornamentation of a flat surface that led to the early development of pargetting. The impressed type of work was usually contained by panels, which filled the spaces between windows or those beside or above the door. The patterns might alternate between two or three choices, but the overall impression was restful and merely a subtle addition of visual interest.

Ironically the busiest working pargeter in the district is embellishing the inter-war bungalows of eastern Essex with free-hand relief pargetting of great elaboration. Existing old pargetted plasterwork is often masked by the thickly textured new kinds of house paint or render: again it was the traditional coat of lime colour wash that best preserved the relics of old work.

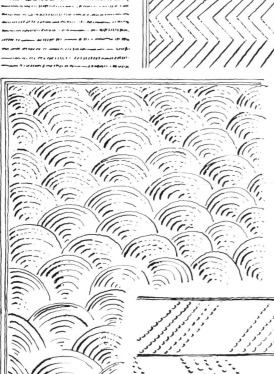

This selection of traditional Suffolk and Essex pargetting patterns were impressed into soft lime plaster which was strengthened with animal hair. Each pattern was set in a panel. The specially designed tools were made from wood. Modern pargetting on hard cement fails to achieve the softer outlines of this earlier work.

This terrace of cottages in Bridge Street, Saffron Walden, Essex has been decorated with pargetting in many designs. The patterns are contained in panels and they have all been incised into the plaster with a specially made instrument. These repetitive geometrical patterns are the designs of traditional pargetting, matching the simplicity of simple cottages such as these, probably of Tudor origin.

This house at Withermarsh Green in Suffolk overlooks a large green, a reminder of the village common land. It is a one and a half storey cottage with substantial brick chimney stacks as a later addition to what was probably a very primitive structure. Inside it still preserves the copper, originally used for heating the water.

While pargetting dies another skill well developed in the eastern counties, thatching, is on the increase. The demand for thatch is considerable and most thatchers are able to justify training apprentices in their trade. Despite the often negative view of insurance companies towards fire risk in thatch, the advantages of it as a roofing material remain considerable. For its climatic versatility, warm in winter, cool in summer, it is as good as modern insulation and the problem of vermin and birds (another objection to thatch in many people's minds) is negligible. In the past a thatcher, like a carpenter, worked in a defined area; defined by the distance he could travel in the day. He developed his own trademarks, usually illustrated by the way he ornamented the ridge. Thatchers generally had an employment fall-back for the winter months, such as making sheep hurdles. Now the sought-after thatchers (for some are better than others) travel throughout a wide district working wherever they are asked to go. Recently a number of British thatchers have been working in the United States where an increasing interest in both vernacular architecture and picturesque neo-vernacular buildings has led to a demand for their abilities. It is the correct quality material for thatching that has become scarce. Combine-harvested straw is bruised in the process and is, in any case, too short. Straw for thatching has to be specially grown and cut, by reaper or binder. It also has to be combed out into a usable form. For that reason, and because they last longer on the roof, water reeds have generally taken over from straw as thatching material.

While thatching and modern derivatives of decorative plasterwork survive, the carpentry tradition associated with fine oak has, inevitably, gone. Similarly no one but an enthusiast, working on his own behalf, is likely to revive the making of clay bat walls when breeze blocks or bricks are available at economic prices. Still, with a good render and the two requisites of a mud wall, a solid, waterproof footing and some form of protection from the elements above, many clay walls survive. Clay lump, or bat, has advantages over cob, since it takes the form of bricks and can therefore be replaced in the same way as deteriorating bricks, a block at a time.

The buildings of Essex and Suffolk take their colours from the surroundings – the different hues of brick, from Suffolk 'white' (greyish yellow, in fact) to the soft reds of the Tudor bricks and specials still being made by hand in a series of old kilns outside Sudbury. The building materials echo shades of earth, straw or timber, and their colours are heightened by the subtle vegetable and mineral tints which enlivened the lime wash as it built up in hundreds of layers over the plaster, giving much needed protection to the walls and the flimsier timbers beneath. Only the recent introduction of harsh chemical paint colours, making no reference to the landscape, has broken up this harmonious cycle of tones.

The picture we see now is a drastically reduced version of the original Tudor built landscape. The majority of buildings of that date and earlier were designed to be built and rebuilt at constant intervals. The rudimentary shelter of the late medieval labourer was of utterly primitive construction and bore as little relationship to the sophisticated domestic architecture of the succeeding period as the classically inspired four-square brick parsonage or farmhouse of the eighteenth century did to its predecessors. Many of the latter though do disguise earlier houses; the passion for refronting rambling late medieval or Tudor houses in the manner of a symmetrical Georgian 'box' was to reach epidemic proportions, here as elsewhere in agriculturally affluent districts. It was another step in the untiring efforts of the independent yeoman class to affirm his status – economic and social. Some of these houses stand on moated sites, emphasising the process of continuity. The vast numbers of such sites throughout East Anglia are the proof of early farm settlements. At that time a corral for the animals against thieving neighbours or at least a good drainage system on heavy water-logged clay soil were necessities. In other cases the moat may have been a result of piling up earth to give a dry platform to the farmhouse and its buildings. However, the moat was not a defence against political turmoil. The East Anglian farmer of late medieval times was not living in an embattled state and the climate of his life was far from that of his counterpart further north: on the borders between Yorkshire and Lancashire such stability was a long time coming to the local inhabitants. In Scotland, the trust between neighbours was to come even later.

Nowadays, the farmhouses and the labourers' cottages of Essex and Suffolk are less and less frequently the homes of those who work, or have any direct connection with the land. Agriculture is becoming a mysterious business and takes place in large, multi-functional sheds – milking parlours, cattle sheds and storage depots all at once. The traditional farm buildings associated with arable agriculture, even the tithe barns built for ecclesiastical and secular land owners to standards not far from those of church and mansion, fall out of use and often into dereliction.

There is new life in and around these traditional structures but often surprisingly distant from their original purposes. New technology and types of manufacturing have brought many farm buildings back into use and the future implications for accessible areas such as this are considerable. The process of change along these lines has been guided by the same common-sense attitudes as those which guided the builders of the past. A continued useful life for the best quality buildings of the countryside seems to pay suitable respect to the masterly craftsmen of those structures; the houses still suit the domestic functions of modern life and the barns and outbuildings, often essentially large, uncluttered sheds, can prove just as useful.

This moated farmhouse at Willingale in Essex is completely encircled by water except for the entrance lane, a familiar pattern throughout this area. The house, though refronted in the eighteenth century, contains remnants of a much earlier building and the site has been built on since the medieval period.

North Norfolk

The traditional practice of cutting and bundling water reeds for thatch is seen here near Salthouse in Norfolk.

If man had set out to find the most awkward, unsuitable building material, he could hardly better flint. Impervious, irregularly shaped, laborious and slow to build and requiring a brick skeleton to hold it together, it seems to defy all the laws of construction and common sense. Its only two obvious advantages are its availability and its decorative possibilities.

In North Norfolk flint is everywhere, and is used at every opportunity in a magnificent variety of finishes, utilising everything from the tiniest pebble or flint chipping to vast amoeboid stones. Nothing could be clearer than the connection between the buildings of the central coast stretch of North Norfolk – farmhouses, cottages, farm buildings, churches and walls – and the ground on which they stand. Flints litter the fields, they lie piled beside sand and gravel pits and they coat the beaches in wide, silvery drifts. The colour range of flint is considerable: where they have been taken directly from the chalk bed they are skinned in a pith of white, in sand they become stained yellow while the sea-washed stones are clear blues, browns and greys. Flints may be knotty, almost anthropomorphic with eyes, noses and limbs, or finely honed to perfect ovals and bead shapes. Thousands of years in the water or ice have rubbed the corners off the most obdurate of stone. Once collected, whether from the shore or a field, each builder worked with the materials as seemed appropriate,

67

according to his skill and preference and, to a lesser extent, to the fashion of the period. Usually the flints were used as found but the most elaborate flintwork required a further refinement, that the stones be split, or knapped, to present a flat and gleaming surface on the exterior. This might be taken further, with the flints worked into squares or circles (known in Norfolk as 'snapped' flints). At its most sophisticated this technique produced the fine ornamentation of fourteenth- and fifteenth-century East Anglian churches known as proudwork and flushwork: the split flints, when they catch the light, give a silky sheen to the otherwise rough texture of weather-beaten stonework.

Sometimes the flint was coursed, carefully graded into rows of matching shapes or sizes, but nowadays, they are most often set random with the projecting part of the flint laid inwards – 'snout down' in the appropriate Norfolk phrase.

Other techniques and decorative finishes include galleting (or garretting) in which little flint chips or even pebbles are laid exposed in the mortar, or the overall use of thousands of tiny flint flakes packed into place, apparently dry but in fact mortared well back, which produces an effect rather like a symmetrical bank of shale. It must have been an astonishingly laborious process and is, not surprisingly, relatively unusual.

In the past, flint walls were constructed as two skins, with rubble filling the cavity. Now flint provides the outer skin, breeze blocks the inner one, and the cavity between is filled with insulating material.

These barns were built of clunch. Chalk and flint are found in the same geological formations and so often turn up in combination. Here the chalk is interspersed with brick and the roofs are of pantiles.

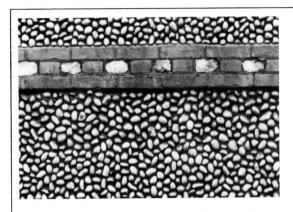

Flint details

Small, rounded beach pebbles (ground down from flints originally) make an optically dazzling wall on cottages in Sheringham (above). A brick string course, with larger flints set in, breaks up the expanse.

The flint on the gable end of this barn at Hunworth (right) is enlivened by brick tumbling, the date and quoins. The odd brick has been dropped in as a device for taking off any moisture which flint, being impermeable, cannot.

These knapped flints (below), with their elaborate flint chip galleting, are at Wiveton Hall. The time-consuming and elaborate ornamentation is proof of the high status of the house.

Chips of chalk-whitened galleting encircle the knapped flints (above) which have been split by a hard tap at the point where someone with an experienced ear can hear it ring.

This wall (below) is on an out-barn on the North Norfolk coast, at Morston. Here, the brick and clunch (chalk) are used in a chequer pattern.

However, modern techniques have provided no quick and easy route to flint construction: it still has to be built a foot or two at a time, with a drying period between each stage. This makes the process a slow one and even by choosing the largest flints and hence cutting down on the labour involved, there are really no short cuts. If the wall is built too fast, and the mortar is still damp when the next stage is added, the wall will bulge out. Wet weather also impedes flint building, though fortunately Norfolk has light rainfall.

To deal with the absorption of moisture, which the impervious flints cannot do, it is necessary that the mortar be of the correct lime and sand consistency; if too hard it merely compounds the problem, for water will force its way around it, particularly under frosty conditions, with dogged persistence. Random bricks set at intervals between the flint can perform a useful service, soaking up the moisture, and the brick footings, bonding and quoins also help in this respect. Flint is a deceptively difficult material to use. Those who understand its properties emphasise how easy it is to produce disastrous results – either by the misapplication of the mortar (which has to be brushed back, with a wooden stick, as a second step) or by overlooking the problem of moisture being trapped in the walls. At a time when full-scale revival in the use of flint is encouraged by planning authorities as being 'in keeping', mistakes are frequently being made, with often unsightly results.

Machine-made bricks are no substitute for the old hand-made Norfolk reds, which were made in village brickworks in the past wherever suitable clay existed. The remnants of brick kilns can still be found dotting the countryside; some of the works were still operational in the 1950s. Now when demand is again high, hand-made bricks are brought in from Suffolk; nobody can provide a Norfolk brick, made from Norfolk clay.

Building in flint, the modern mason cannot follow the escape route chosen by some of his medieval forebears. They, daunted by the prospect of achieving right-angled corners without the use of either limestone or brick quoins to tie in the stonework, expediently built circular church towers, a happy example of necessity proving to be the mother of invention.

Traditionally the life of North Norfolk people has revolved around agriculture and fishing – the two are often combined along the coast. Farming shifted from the medieval emphasis on large sheep runs towards arable agriculture which was well suited to this dry, low-lying landscape. Late medieval life revolved around a fully developed manorial system; it has been estimated that in the early fourteenth century there were at least 1400 manor houses in Norfolk. When the manors began to lose their dominance in the social order of the area, the manor houses often moved down the social scale to become tenanted farmhouses. Many were rebuilt or at least remodelled in the Tudor and Jacobean periods, while some were shifted to new sites.

This brick threshing barn at Guist bears a datestone 1723. The stepped gables and perforated ventilation 'windows' show the confidence of the local builders with bricks which had once been a luxury material. The owl hole at the apex provided exit and entry for that efficient vermin exterminator. The wooden doors are for pitching straw down from the upper level loft.

Wiveton Hall commands a fine position on a headland opposite Cley next the Sea. Although now separated from it by marshes and water meadows, when the house was built in 1652, Cley was a considerable port. Wiveton Hall follows the pattern of Norfolk manor houses with the Tudor E-plan becoming an H. Here the shaped gables and pedimented windows, made of brick in a largely flint house, add Jacobean flourishes to an essentially Tudor house.

In North Norfolk the manor houses and halls are built of flint and brick – although for some time humble cottages and hovels in the surrounding village would still have been constructed of timber frames with mud panels between. Their larger neighbours, the Tudor or Jacobean manor houses, were built with one eye on the new mansions of the most influential families in the land, scaled down according to the relatively modest requirements of the local land-owner. While the Tudor E-plan had been a reminder of earlier enclosed courtyard plans, the simpler Norfolk house, with its slightly projecting side bays and impressive, storeyed-over porch was a pared away version of the 'E' with the porch as a relic of the gatehouse. Often the staircase was also housed in its own gabled extension.

After the Dissolution some manors were built or rebuilt with canni-balised materials wrested from the ruined abbeys and monastic estab-lishments. For example, Abbey Farm, North Creake, was built in the cloisters of the abbey after an epidemic wiped out the monks in 1506: despite subsequent changes and a complete refronting in the early nineteenth century, mullioned and traceried windows and other clues internally and externally point to the origins of the house. By an ironic twist, it is disused farm buildings that now provide the second-hand materials for a new generation of buildings – holiday cottages, converted barns and new housing estates with their obli-gatory nod to the vernacular of the region.

Although flint and brick in combination were to remain the favoured material for the larger houses of North Norfolk, brick used alone was exploited to provide some impressive and elaborate results, most notably at East Barsham Hall, an extraordinary confection of contorted chimneys, battlements and pinnacles rising out of its site in a steeply folded valley. Rich men in these parts were in close contact with Europe and fashionable Flemish and French influences came early to the eastern extremities of England. An elaborate brick barn, such as that at Guist, is a descendant of such houses.

The Low Countries provided that other utterly characteristic Norfolk building material – used for great houses and simple farm buildings alike – the pantile. The steep pitch of the roofs of the seventeenth-century houses in North Norfolk indicates that they were constructed to take thatch, which requires that angle in order that it will drain effectively. Reeds along the coastal marshes, river banks and on the Norfolk Broads further east provided the raw material. Nowadays, Norfolk reeds are cut in the winter months and are used widely in the eastern and southern parts of the county and throughout the southern counties, but for North Norfolk itself, only pantiles are to be seen.

The first type of tile to be used was a pin-tile, so-called as a derivation from plain tiles, but these were superseded by the pantile which appeared in eastern England in the seventeenth century. Originally the pantile was imported from the Netherlands, a visible sign of the strong trade links established with that country, and the tiles often came in as cargo on returning wool boats. The tiles were laid on a kind of underfelt of reeds, which provided insulation but did not interfere with the ventilation which pantiles ensure with their curved form. Wherever trade links were made with the Continent, as far north as Whitby in Yorkshire or further south down to the Waveney Valley into Suffolk, pantiles can be found – usually matt, tomato-coloured, but from time to time glazed black giving an oriental lacquer to the roofscape of the towns or villages. The elaboration of the steep gables, either in series of brick steps or curving into curlicues of coping, is another characteristic of North Norfolk buildings – again an echo of architectural practices from the Netherlands.

Down the social scale, the cottages in the tightly clustered villages of the rich farmland inland of the coastal marshes were, by the seventeenth and early eighteenth centuries, almost universally built of flint and brick; timber framing had gone and local brick had replaced the time-consuming construction of wall panels of mud and straw. Varying little, the one-and-a-half or two-storey cottages provided a couple of rooms up, a couple down. However, going west the dominant building material alters, with surprising suddenness, from flint to clunch and then it changes again, on the western coast going south to Kings Lynn, to that curious fudge-coloured stone, carr stone, by turns the most mellow or the most obtrusive of building materials.

In his *Afoot in England*, W.H. Hudson wrote of his impressions of carr stone: 'an orange-brown stone found in the neighbourhood, the roofs being all of hard, black slate. I had never seen houses of such a colour; it was stronger, more glaring and aggressive than the reddest brick ...'. Nevertheless, used in irregular blocks, with a cream mortar sometimes peppered with chips of flint, the old stone walls or simple cottages built from carr stone in the seventeenth or early eighteenth centuries share nothing of Hudson's description, they look far closer to the golden ironstones of Northamptonshire, about which no writers have ever complained.

Although all three areas are still distinct, it is only in the flint area that attempts have been made in recent years to keep, or to revive, the practice of using the available stone. Chalk is occasionally used in repairs and requires considerable expertise to use it to best advantage, whilst carr stone, still quarried at Snettisham, is widely used as a foundation material since it compacts easily. Its awkward characteristics, odd appearance and unpleasant look when used with modern brick have ensured that it is rarely used for walls.

This small, double-fronted cottage of one and a half storeys is at Field Dalling. Its gabled porch and pedimented windows are unusually elaborate features for such an early, and humble, brick, flint and pantiled cottage.

On the north coast the climate and the seasons have determined an opportunistic way of life, still followed by a number of the local people. By turns they fish, cut reeds, dig for bait in the sand or mud flats or do odd building jobs. The houses, built where possible out of reach of freak tides and floods, turn their backs on the north-easterly gales and the double-skinned flint has ensured hefty walls. Huddled coastal villages, such as Cley, Blakeney or Salthouse, show very different faces to the mid-summer tourist and the mid-winter visitor, who may find deep sea mist or, if fortunate, clear skies, blond acres of reeds and the vivid russet of the tiled roofs which are visible for miles.

A good number of the simple terraced or semi-detached cottages in Blakeney, which line the roadside down to the quay or form little culs-de-sac off to one side or another, have small metal plaques identifying them as the property of the Blakeney Neighbourhood Housing Association. This was founded after the last war by a local woman who realised that rising house prices, because of competition from retired people and holiday-makers, were driving out the local

The disused stables around which these crab pots are stored at Cley next the Sea, are an example of the high-quality Victorian flintwork that was incorporated into both domestic and utilitarian buildings while labour was cheap and the materials readily available.

population altogether. The twenty-two houses of the Association now perform a double function: they have helped keep Blakeney people in the village and also ensured the survival of the traditional fabric of the place. The cottages, which in the late 1940s cost about £200 each, would now be selling at inflated prices but under this system they are let for fair rents to people with proven connections with Blakeney. Mostly late eighteenth- or early nineteenth-century flint cottages, their simple lines are a welcome corrective to the often involved 'improvements' wrought on the plain, utilitarian houses of the coast around here.

Despite inroads made by standardised materials in the mid-nineteenth century, it still continued to make sense (along the Norfolk coast) to take building materials from the most obvious place – the beach. At the height of the fishing industry, which came to its peak here in the late nineteenth century, the last generation of flint fishermen's cottages were put up in Sheringham. They were purpose-built, often in detached pairs, linked by a communal passageway in which nets and gear could be stored, and sometimes lived in by

These cottages in Sheringham were built of beach pebbles, smaller and rounder than field flints. These were once fishermen's cottages. The villa in the foreground is a late Victorian or Edwardian addition – considerably more elaborate than the earlier traditional terrace to the left.

members of different branches of the same family. Outbuildings behind offered the space for storage of crab pots and a place to work on the nets and pots in the winter months when little or no fishing took place. Rounded beach pebbles double for the walls of the house and the paving and were often collected off the beach by the women, while the men built the cottages. Only since the last war has the gathering of flints from the beach been forbidden, although after they were no longer gathered as building materials they were still collected by the sackful to go to the Potteries. The ground flints added body and lightened the china clay. Flint was also used to provide the silica content in early glass making. Moving the pebbles weakened the sea defences and increased the stress on the sea walls so removal of them was banned. Nevertheless, by the forces of variable tides and prevailing winds, a curious sorting process goes on; one tide will bring in great boulder-sized pebbles, another, millions of tiny ones.

The fishermen's cottages are now, with few exceptions, holiday homes. The fishing industry as such is almost gone: a tiny handful of boats operates out of these North Norfolk ports, a fraction of the number of even thirty years ago. As fishing continues to retreat in the face of large-scale enterprises, both from home and abroad, leaving only the prospect of part-time crabbing or herring fishing, tourism has replaced it. It is nothing new for these coastal places: one writer commented in 1909 that the residents 'awoke to the fact that they might garner another harvest besides those of the fields and sea and now the railway has made them popular'. Cromer, Sheringham and resorts of different types, catering for different interests, have all absorbed the summer visitors. The local people have doubtless forgiven Clarence Scott, Edwardian author of *Poppyland*, whose vivid picture of the charms of North Norfolk, and its poppy-rimmed cliffs and fields, encouraged a whole industry of poppy-ornamented souvenirs. Now the tourists remain and the poppies have fallen victim to modern agriculture.

It is now the inland, agricultural villages that are feeling the impact of the visitor. With many of the coastal villages fully exploited or else strictly controlled against further development, the brunt of the continuing influx of tourists is felt far from the sight or sound of the sea. Ranges of disused farm buildings, often a complete, inward-facing courtyard of barn and associated animal sheds, readily convert into holiday 'flatlets' or cottages. This avoids certain restrictions on building and, at best, such conversions can be unobtrusive. More satisfactory for the economic health and the external appearance of the area, perhaps, is the idea of turning these types of buildings into industrial premises requiring less alteration to the fabric and, additionally, to the function. Such complexes at Langham and Glandford have been well treated and, in addition, have given some jobs back to the local population, replacing those lost as farm labour has contracted.

Valley Farm, Gunthorpe (right), is a typical Norfolk manor farmhouse with a gabled stairblock and a porch on the opposite side. It is built of flint, brick and pantiles and dates from the seventeenth century.

Stiffkey Hall was built in the 1570s and is an early example of a grand house built with flint in Northamptonshire. The corner towers are a reminder of the problem of making an angle with flint. It was easier to build circular structures.

Outlying threshing barns, such as these near Ringstead, north-west Norfolk (above), with fold yards for cattle, are a feature of the post Agricultural Revolution landscape.

This tiny double cottage (left) was built during the seventeenth-century rebuilding of Wadenhoe village in Northamptonshire. The earlier medieval village is a series of hummocks around the parish church.

Farm buildings are the most noticeable modern structures in the North Norfolk countryside, often functioning as great all-purpose warehouses in contrast to the carefully linked and specialised functions of the vernacular buildings that characterised the traditional farmsteads of this agriculturally rich area. Many of these new sheds are badly sited and ugly; they require no planning permission. Some might say that it is fitting that in the birthplace of the Agricultural Revolution – the home of Turnip Townsend and Thomas Coke – agricultural buildings both new and old are providing the fabric of the future. Nevertheless, the resilient character of the Norfolk people, not so far from the flint of their buildings, makes it hard to believe that North Norfolk will become an occasional staging-post for its visitors to the exclusion of all else. To the contrary, a new, young population is moving in with the sole objective of living and working on the spot. In some cases it is these people, 'outsiders' of a different kind, who are reviving old skills and suggesting that the traditional ways of life, modified in line with the late twentieth century, are in many respects the most appropriate in such an area. The vernacular buildings are, to a large extent, the most obvious link between that past and this present.

North-East Northamptonshire

The village of Nassington in Northamptonshire is seen from across the surrounding fields.

The landscape of Midland England, as it is found in north-eastern Northamptonshire, has its own dramatic qualities. Light flicking across the landscape illuminates the bright whiteness of the limestone church spires and surrounding buildings to an almost electric intensity. The verticals of soaring spires look like a conscious attempt on the part of medieval builders to direct attention upwards from the unremitting flatness of the countryside. There are valleys here, and shallow hills, but they hardly puncture the gently undulating horizons. The beauty of the landscape is close to the ground, in its wealth of buildings, virtually all of stone, and in its emphatic expanse of skies as backcloth.

There are no outcrops or rocky excrescences here. The oolitic limestone, the hidden asset of this corner of the Midlands, is a continuation of the so-called Stone-Belt, which runs from the south west, in the Cotswolds, up to Humberside in the north east. This milky grey stone has provided the materials for a rich traditional architecture, less well recognised than its Cotswold neighbour but hardly less magnificent as found in the close-knit villages and small towns along the valleys of the Nene or the Welland. It is easy to tell where the stone lies. The transition above ground, from stone to brick, happens from one village to the next. The area lies to the east of the central watershed, so that its rivers run to the east coast and it

Haunt Hill House, Great Weldon (above), is a small house with some unusually elaborate features since it was built by a family of masons for their own use. It is of Weldon stone – a limestone quarried nearby. It has datestones of 1636, 1643 and 1719.

Two-storeyed canted bays can be seen on this house (top right) dated 1640, in Oundle. It is built of local oolitic limestone.

This terrace of stone cottages in Wadenhoe (right) has the traditional hipped dormers and wooden lintels over the windows.

is along these routes that the stone travelled out and, to a lesser extent, pantiles travelled in. Limestone provided a roofing material too; the fissured sandy limestone mined at Collyweston competes with the Oxfordshire equivalent which protected roofs further west. Not far away ironstone provided the perfect foil for the cool shades of the locally quarried limestones: a vibrant orange, it is sometimes banded in courses and sometimes used for quoins or dressings on the elevations of the prosperous manorial farmhouses which are to be found in almost every village here. The juxtaposition of the two stones was one way to ring the changes: another was the personal choice of the mason, his preferred procedure given the material. Some used the stone random, that is without attempting to match or cut the blocks to a relative uniformity. Some used it in regular courses, while later and better quality buildings tended to be built of ashlared freestone with neat, chalky mortar sometimes jazzed up with tiny fragments of black grit to give the effect – intentional or not – of galleting. It helped compact the mortar too.

The masons of Northamptonshire and the surrounding area began to establish their own hallmarks. As in other stone-built areas where a strong vernacular developed, confident enough to sustain such features as the Cotswold dormer, the ornamented lintel of the north-west Pennines, or the heavy window surrounds of the area to either side of the Solway Firth, distinct regional variations can be identified. The twin shaft chimney stacks, tied by coping at the rim, and canted bays with strong mullions are two features frequently

This thatch and limestone cottage in Wakerley has a 45° pitch roof designed specifically for thatch. The thatch is pulled down over the attic windows, giving the cottage its characteristically cosy image.

found here. Hipped dormers, deeply modelled drip moulds and plain doorways are further characteristics found in the villages built as Rockingham Forest was cleared, or those in the manorial strongholds a little to the south.

The prolonged period of relative wealth which gave rise to that phenomenon now known as the Great Rebuilding of Elizabethan and Jacobean times allowed and encouraged the masons of the Cotswolds or here further along the same belt of limestone continually to refine their skills and to share them with those who built the humblest of cottages or simple barns or sheds – the category of building in which the vernacular details that had been long since outmoded or forgotten in 'polite' architecture lingered on. Thus, for example, the mullioned window which had disappeared in the face of the wooden sash or casement window was still being inserted in unpretentious houses in the late seventeenth and even into the eighteenth centuries.

The Northamptonshire scene still accurately reflects the forces which formed it: its buildings and their sites are the most graphic illustration of the series of events and, often, great changes and reverses which modelled the landscape. Those have included dramatic depopulation, at two periods prior to the building of the existing villages – one was during the Plague which in the mid-fourteenth century claimed vast numbers of the population and the second, more insidious, was the effect of enclosures. The importance of the latter in terms of removing the landless population from the prosperous agricultural acreages of the east Midlands can be gauged from Maurice Beresford's estimate that Northampton was the county which carried out the highest number of prosecutions for depopulation through enclosure between 1517 and 1565.

The agricultural pattern inherited from medieval times was open-field cultivation: strip cultivation of manorial lands was carried out by landless labourers who had access to considerable common and waste lands for their own use. Enclosure, particularly in the sixteenth century, was a result of the landlords breaking up this system and replacing it with great sheep-grazing ranches, effectively dispossessing the labourers and providing them with little or no compensation. Later enclosure, carried out in the eighteenth century by private acts of Parliament, took this reordering of the land a stage further, though this time the land was enclosed primarily for arable use in order to carry out the new and efficient practices of the Agricultural Revolution.

Thus the built landscape of Northamptonshire is made up of tightly nucleated villages rather than the scattered pattern of individual farmsteads which obtains in the south west and elsewhere, in areas where the land ownership is divided between large numbers of independent owner-occupiers, yeoman, or statesman as they were known in some regions, and where the political unit is the parish.

The villages which line up along the Nene and Welland valleys, and elsewhere in many other parts of the east Midlands, reflect a long history of mixed agriculture. When enclosures replaced open-field agriculture, the grouping of farms within the village centre seemed still to make good sense. Some villages were being entirely rebuilt; earlier foundations, often marked by an isolated parish church at some distance from the present site, were completely abandoned after decimation of the population either by disease or rapacious landlords. That depopulation was followed by new, relatively ordered development. A village green, scant restitution for the lost common lands, a central street and an often distinguished manor farmhouse were the focal points. In some cases, there might be a grander house, a mansion denoting the landowner as someone probably recently rewarded for services to the Crown, and then the ranks of cottages, secondary farms and outbuildings were added as the seventeenth and eighteenth centuries progressed. Almshouses and sometimes an endowed school were added as proof of the responsibilities felt by the proprietor of a village. A complex, dependent village society was built up, expressed by its buildings – first church, then manorial privilege, were the determining influences.

A good example of this process, well preserved to this day, is the village of Wadenhoe, south of Oundle. Mounds in a field close to the Norman parish church are an eloquent reminder of the earlier village.

Three typical kinds of roof covering can be seen here in this Wadenhoe scene. There is a row of thatched cottages, beyond that a stone tiled farmhouse and a pantiled structure on the far right.

The present village, with a green surrounded by terraced cottages of various dates up to the mid-nineteenth century, and a main street which takes a direct route downhill and then splits to reach the River Nene by two lanes, one to the mill and the other to the riverside inn, is predominantly of the seventeenth and eighteenth centuries. It is built of limestone, taken from two quarries just outside the village which have long ago passed out of use. The roofs are a cross-section of the available materials – thatch, stone slates and pantiles.

The oldest house in the village appears to be the Manor Farm, with an internal beam dated 1593 and two plaster overmantels upstairs which have the pattern of stubby arcading that looks more sixteenth century than seventeenth. Despite these details, the house was obviously remodelled, at least once, not long after and datestones on the exterior of the house, 1653 and 1670, must refer to that. Like so many of the larger manorial farmhouses in the district, it is a T-shaped house. Sometimes houses were built double-pile, so that the line of the roof resembles an 'M', with a valley between two identical blocks built back to back. That symmetrical pattern is widely found in the Cotswolds and in the stone villages of Oxfordshire. The Manor Farm at Wadenhoe has a lop-sided arrangement of windows on its roadside face, but closer examination suggests that the windows at the lower end of the house had been blocked for Window Tax. The blocked windows were turned into shallow cupboards in the eighteenth century, so that internally it is easy to see where they were.

This house, a typical example of the kind of well-constructed, pleasantly proportioned larger farmhouse of the area, is set in front of a group of farmbuildings, the dominant structure of which is a solidly built stone threshing barn. There is also a nineteenth-century addition, a small detached brew-house, a relic of a time when farms would supply their own requirements for ale and possibly pay part of the labourers' wages by this means.

Manorial rights were a complex web of legal and customary rights, some of which have survived to this day. The one privilege which proved particularly irksome to the neighbours of the Lord of the Manor, or his representative, was that of keeping pigeons. The dove-cote provided an important source of fresh meat the year round and it stands as a reminder of the problems of provisioning for a full year in the centuries before cold storage or concentrated foodstuffs for livestock made little of the problem. At Wadenhoe, a magnificent 2000 nesting-box circular dovecote stands in one of the manorial farmyards, each box of lath and plaster, with a full-height pivotal ladder so that the egg collector could reach into every one of the boxes. Now that the dovecote is empty of the sounds and smells of pigeons it is hard to imagine the scene but it is easy to understand the trepidation of villagers whose meagre vegetable gardens could be laid waste at a stroke by a visit of even a few dozen of the birds.

The Manor Farm at Wadenhoe is a T-shaped house. It originally had many more windows on this side but they were presumably blocked off to evade Window Tax. The chimney stacks repeat the local pattern. The small building to the right is a brewhouse.

This manorial
dovecote in Wadenhoe is
built of limestone and
tiled in stone slates.

Wadenhoe has been in the hands of the same family since around 1700. Some years ago they became concerned for the future of the village, which has remained remarkably complete architecturally, and has been respectfully maintained to a high standard. To this end a large part of the village was handed over to the care of a charitable trust whose trustees will have responsibility for its future. The village is now secure from the vagaries of sudden heavy taxation, the selling of open space for development or the deterioration that too often happens when owners will neither sell nor repair properties. The object of this step is to preserve the architectural character and to ensure the continuation of a living village, certainly not to fossilise the place.

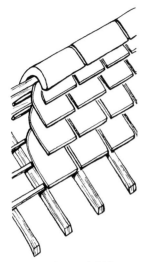

Slate roofs were laid in diminishing courses (above), and capped by U-shaped ridge tiles.

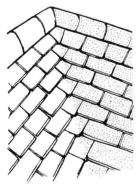

At the angle between the roof surfaces, the tiler had to invent a method of turning the corner. This involved cutting the stones into diamond shapes.

Around Wadenhoe, in villages such as Stoke Doyle or Titchmarsh, or, north of Oundle, Cotterstock on the River Nene, Barrowden and Harringworth on the River Welland, the pattern of agriculture remains much as it has been for centuries – sheep and corn. Sheep provided the wealth upon which many of the more sizeable towns were built, Oundle or King's Cliffe for example, while Stamford, further north, is one of the great wool towns of England. Grain provided a *raison d'être* for breweries and mills: the river valleys are dotted with fine eighteenth- and nineteenth-century water mills, one to a village, which processed the rich harvest of this open, dry land and brought in more wealth. The water meadows along the river banks, often flooded, made ideal year-round grazing and from Stilton, nearby, came one of the most famed English cheeses. Mixed agriculture tended historically to lead to bigger holdings, although they did not compare with the size of farms today.

The rivers were the means of transport for the stone which served the immediate vicinity and was transported throughout eastern England for the important buildings – churches, mansions, tithe barns – from the medieval period onwards. Quarries such as Weldon (just closed down) and Ketton, and beyond Stamford, Barnack and Clipsham, provided some of the best stone available in the country. Although the small village quarries that added to this supply have ceased to operate and in many cases have disappeared without trace beneath the turf, the famous names are still in business. The stone slates for which Collyweston is so famous present a more considerable problem, for without harsh winters they cannot be split, and although people have toyed with refrigeration as a more reliable substitute, most Collyweston slating depends on second-hand stone and thus on the disintegration of buildings somewhere in the area.

Collyweston slates dictated the form of the roofs on which they were laid. Because they are irregular, they need to be set at a steep pitch in order to throw off rain water, and their considerable weight requires a hefty timber frame beneath. They are traditionally laid in diminishing courses, the largest at the eaves, the smallest at the ridge. The valleys, as for example between a dormer and the main roof expanse, are not flashed with lead but are carefully tiled either by specially cut diamond-shaped stones or by an elegant interlocking of slates of the right size. These roofs, in Alec Clifton-Taylor's phrase 'the crowning touch of harmony' on the buildings, are covered by peat-coloured moss and silver-grey lichen, and are harmonious neighbours to thatch of wheat or water reed (both are used in Northamptonshire), which also requires a steep pitch of roof.

The dexterity with which the builders of farmhouses, barns and cottages dealt with the stone is considerable. To provide ventilation in barns, for example, the builders would carefully provide a slit, dressed as elaborately as if it were a domestic window, or even a little triangular vent. The barns and houses of these tightly centred villages

The row of limestone cottages (left) leads up the lane to the church in Barrowden.

The Welland viaduct (below) runs in an impressive arc down the valley and is evidence of that most important event in the history of traditional building – the arrival by rail of industrially made materials from far away. It was the end of the predominance of local materials for local buildings.

line up along the road, presenting a largely unrelieved surface of fine stonework to the outside world. The villages have an imperturbable air about them: even the extraordinary marching line of arches forming the Welland viaduct, which carries the railway into the Leicestershire countryside, sidesteps the villages of Gretton and Harringworth. It was the railway, of course, which cracked the hold that the local stone and stone tiles had as building materials. With it came industrial bricks from Bedfordshire or Leicestershire, slates from Wales and so it spelt the beginning of the end for the small village quarry. Nevertheless, these Northamptonshire villages fought off the new materials quite successfully; they are still predominantly built of stone and despite some recent housing developments of reconstituted stone, the blend of vernacular buildings with later developments is a happy one. Many villages retain their character as a result of a long period in single ownership and it is the future for these 'closed' villages that seems uncertain, unless options such as that followed by Wadenhoe can be found. These villages reflect the ordered life under the protection of the feudal system. It is not a picture which accords easily with late twentieth-century life and yet it is the means by which the homogeneity and appeal of the stone villages of eastern Northamptonshire have remained, in many cases, intact.

Southern Snowdonia

This shale-built barn is situated near Lake Tal-y-llyn in North Wales.

Mountains, as forbidding, bold and beautiful as any in Britain, are the key to north-west Wales. They have dictated the conditions of life there: movement, settlement and agriculture have all been strictly limited. The mountains have provided the rock and slate for building, and the poor thin soil for agriculture. They have ensured a climate of high rainfall and frequent mist and cloud and divided the Welsh of north-west Wales from those of the south and east. They have defended and separated the people here from avaricious invaders or interfering outsiders. Finally, in themselves, the mountains of Snowdonia have lured visitors to the area – from the eighteenth-century Romantic traveller in search of *frisson* from their terrifying heights and depths to an equally impressed, if less emotional, twentieth-century visitor.

Apart from the main passes, most of the valleys here are merely timid inroads into the flanks of the rock mass, the tracks which lead to outlying farms and distant grazing petering out in the face of the mountainside. The mountain chain dictated which direction the population traditionally faced and in the valleys and along the seaboard which looks to Dolgellau as the main town, that direction was always westerly, towards the Atlantic and the Irish Sea. Gwynedd and Powys, though neighbouring counties in Wales, have little in common historically.

This farmhouse, barn and dry-stone wall (above) are to be found on the coast between Barmouth and Harlech. Here the rock is one of the most ancient geological formations – Cambrian – and the landscape shares the same durable qualities.

A fine example of a slate roof is to be found at Hafod Dywyll below Cader Idris (right). The farmhouses in the area are uniformly built of local stone and roofed in slate, as here, carefully laid in diminishing courses.

Nevertheless, despite the remoteness and the physical obstacles between Snowdonia and England, the political agreements made between Wales and England, culminating in the sixteenth-century Acts of Union, allowed for an exchange of ideas. Even in this hard-pressed corner of Wales, the stability and prosperity which was already evident in Tudor times expressed itself in buildings and the lineage of some of these structures was clearly connected with neighbouring English counties. As elsewhere, the Black Death in the fourteenth century brought about a complete shift of balance. As a result there was an abundance of land and a desperate shortage of labour. The landless peasant gained independence; the substantial small farmer was born; the manorial system was largely dismantled.

By the sixteenth century, Merioneth was able to boast one of the highest per capita incomes outside London. That impressive achievement was possible with a small population and a considerable wealth based on wool. There was no alternative to sheep farming here, although dairying played its part and, of necessity, every farm had to be self-sufficient in arable crops. It was in the heyday of dairying, in the medieval period, that the system of transhumance became a feature of life. In summer, the farmer and his animals retired to a 'hafod', a farmhouse on higher ground, from which he could find fresh grazing and, Peter Smith suggests in *Houses of the Welsh Countryside* (1975), have a recuperative break from the insanitary conditions and routine of home life. The remainder of the year was spent in a house on lower ground, the 'hendre'. Once the emphasis shifted

Cedris, a farm in the
valley near Tal-y-llyn, is
whitewashed though this
is more unusual here
than in mid-Wales or
other parts of the country
where building in stone is
customary.

firmly to sheep, who require no special housing and far less attention, the practice died out. Travellers noticed it occasionally in Snowdonia as late as the eighteenth century, but effectively it was no more. Transhumance determined aspects of the buildings of the area and is commemorated still in farmhouse names – both dot the maps thickly. Sheep, who brought wealth to the Welsh farmer from the Tudor period onwards, dictated local industry. Fulling mills, depending on water power, tanning, and the breeding of fatstock, were all contributory. The visitor today is forcibly reminded of this past as the loaded lorries speed with their cargoes of fleeces to the Wool Marketing Board grading centre at Dinas Mawddwy or as the pungent aroma of the fellmongers' works (the preliminary stages to tanning) envelopes Dolgellau from two directions. In the past, fat-stock animals were taken on the drovers' routes to better pasture on the Borders or even in southern England. Today the practice continues, though the method of transportation is by lorry and not on foot.

As in East Anglia or the Cotswolds, sheep brought money and that money bought a new way of life. Domestic prosperity from the Tudor period onwards ensured improved domestic conditions: a population of prosperous peasants and those who, in English terms, would be termed yeoman farmers were able to build upon the late medieval tradition of the hall house and construct for themselves housing and outbuildings of superior quality and considerable comfort. The hall house – in its simplest form a single cell, in its more elaborate shape consisting of a main space with subsidiaries at either end – was floored over and a chimney inserted, usually tacked onto the side wall. A stone stair might also be built wrapped around the large chimney breast.

Rich in oak, the timber-framed buildings of the old county of Merioneth share with the north-west of England, Lancashire for example, the sublimely satisfactory structural system of the cruck frame. This is evident in the best early hall houses and in many of the humble barns of the area but, in common with the border counties, the rising cost and increasing scarcity of good timber in the seventeenth century ensured a shift to stone construction, with load-bearing walls.

Merioneth is a county littered with stone: the weathered, rounded grey boulders of the coastal area, the awkward granite blocks quarried from the mid-nineteenth century, and the shale and slate. These stones were either there for the asking, or readily available from the quarries and mines which proliferated to service a rising population requiring durable buildings. From its roots in the immediate locality, the production of building materials for a far wider market became an industry, culminating in the nineteenth century with the slate industry, which was centred on towns such as Blaenau Ffestiniog or Bethesda, further north, which supplied the roofs of an empire.

Field barns, such as this one set against an outcrop of rock near Llanbedr, were necessary in an area where farms were widely spread and animals needed shelter and fodder during the hard times of the year.

The appearance of the smaller houses, cottages and farm buildings of this area was largely determined by the nature of the available materials. The vast boulders that formed the foundations and acted as corner stones, effectively bracing any eccentric stresses in the building, are one of the characteristic features of the traditional building style here. Diminishing slightly as the walls rise, the overall effect is, nevertheless, one of massive bulk, even if the building in question is simply a field barn. In more sophisticated examples, similar boulders are used as lintels to door or window and slate slabs pave the way to the door. Given the realities of the climate, the combination of hefty blocks of stone, which do not require the skills of a mason to fashion them, with the chips of shale or slate that are used to infill the blocks or deflect the rainfall, is a rather fortuitous one. The 'weather stones', as the slate steps on gable or chimney stack which protect any vulnerable joints from the endless onslaught of rainwater are known, are a characteristic feature shared in some other north-western areas, in particular Cumbria, where similar conditions prevail.

In the eighteenth century travellers noticed how, in addition to the joints between boulders being plugged with small stones, turf and peat were also used as a kind of mortar. Though there are few instances of such dry-stone walling now (beyond the characteristic field walls which, especially along the coast, make a tight tapestry pattern punctuated by the barns and farms themselves) the pointing was traditionally discreet and one of the sad modern disfigurements of buildings here is the tendency to over-point with heavy cement mortar. Though rough-cast render and a coat of whitewash is many people's idea of a 'typically Welsh' building finish, in this part of the country it was used sparingly, often only to protect the most exposed wall of the house or to mask less well-built work. The walls were often built of double skins to keep them dry, with the space between filled with rubble, mortar or even bran. Roofs which today are most commonly covered in symmetrical courses of blue-black slates were traditionally thatched with reed or straw laid over wattle. The high chimney stacks of some of the ancient farmhouses is proof of that fact. However, thatch gave way to stone slates in many areas quite early and the diminishing courses of stone slates, sometimes seeded with moss, is one of the disappearing traditional finishes of the area. Elaborate valleys were made to overcome the lack of lead flashings or sealants. These slates were fixed with wooden pegs: their disappearance was already being lamented in 1908 when the authors of *Old Cottages of Snowdonia* wrote that 'after a while it was found to be a saving of time to the slater, though more expensive in initial cost, to get the slates all cut to fixed sizes in the quarry. And though at first they retained their small and thick qualities these were soon replaced by the thin and weak first quality slates, which, though very skilfully split, have done more to ruin the beauty of England and Wales, than

With the consistently high rainfall in Wales, Welsh builders had to use certain materials to provide waterproofing. Here, on a cottage in Dolgelau, chunks of slate or shale provide jutting platforms from which rain water is deflected, leaving the junction between chimney stack and roof less exposed.

even corrugated iron or terra-cotta!' It was the careful gradations of the stonework courses below, and above these the slates, that gave the simple, dormered cottage of eighteenth-century Wales its particular charm.

The valleys and the coastal areas abound with good houses, preserving in many cases the oak post and panel partitions or the cusped roof timbers and high-quality carpentry work. An ostensibly simple farmhouse from the outside, such as Hafod Ysbyty, is revealed internally to be a medieval hall of the fourteenth or fifteenth century, sandwiched between a bay, which was probably the dairy and parlour, and an outer room of two bays, apparently a byre. The magnificence of its ornamented cruck-framed roof points to its importance at the time of building. Early seventeenth-century remodelling included the insertion of a vast chimney and a stair and the flooring over of the hall, as well as the addition of a kitchen block at right angles. Hidden down endless tracks and gated roads far above Ffestiniog, it is typical of the secret sites in which so many of the best buildings in Wales hide. Hardly less well hidden in a gentle valley near the village of Llanfachreth is the house Cae'r March. The adjacent barn turns out to be an even more perfect example of a late medieval hall house, complete with remnants of hammer beams, and without a floor interposed to change the scale. Many other houses have been preserved by similar shifts of fortune: living on as barns there has been little interference in their basic fabric and so nothing material has happened to change their features.

Change is an important ingredient in the form of the Welsh farmhouse. Over the centuries, the basic longhouse or single-roomed cottage has become inadequate; some were built literally overnight in order to gain squatter's rights to the land. A room or a small wing consisting of one room or two, has been added, and then maybe a century or more later, further rooms. Many houses are veritable onions – layer upon layer of skin can be removed. Often the end result is so puzzling or so altered that the stages cannot be unravelled. Just outside Dolgellau, the house Gwanas, a solid Victorian villa at first glance, turns out to have a porch which is a relic of a thirteenth-century hospice, and part of the outbuildings behind it were once a single-roomed longhouse – known in Wales as a 'one chimney house'. It is the chimney that gives the clue to previous human habitation in many byres and barns.

Even the more sophisticated, anglicised model of the classical eighteenth-century house is rarely what it seems. By the river Cader, on the south-west tip of the Cader Idris range, is Cae'rberllan. This impressive farmhouse, with stepped gables, sash windows and an upper dormered storey, is quite honest about its origins. The timber of the roof, and much of the internal detail proclaims it as sixteenth century, and it has 1590 over the door: it also has a datestone recording a rebuilding in 1757.

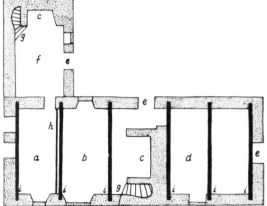

Hafod Ysbyty, near Ffestiniog, gives little away from the outside but its plain appearance disguises an exceptionally fine medieval hall house. The roof is a cruck-framed structure, with five bays, and in the hall the exposed cruck truss is arch-braced with cusping (top). There is a post and panel dais partition between the hall and the inner room, the latter was probably once the dairy and parlour. Behind the chimney stack was a two-bay barn and byre. The stone chimney, the upper floor and the stairs leading to it were added, with the cross wing, around 1600.

a) inner room
b) hall
c) hearth
d) barn and byre
e) entrances
f) cross wing
g) stairs
h) dais partition
i) roof timbers

Cae'rbellan, in the Cader Valley, is surrounded by rich pastures. Beneath the house is a cellar hollowed out of the rock.

This house, in a valley of rare lushness for this corner of Wales, was sited with the dual objectives of allowing easy access to and from the valley and a viewpoint from a slight rise in the ground. Since the valley bottom is flat and the hillsides provide the shelter, other considerations were probably less crucial. But if the Welsh house builder had one consummate art, it is that of choosing the perfect site. In many obviously ancient locations it must have been a carefully considered operation. Many farmhouses benefit from a micro-climate with the temperature, prevailing winds and even rainfall substantially kinder in that spot on which they stand than in an exposed

position a mile or two away. The houses are built well into the side of the hill, neither too high nor too close to the bottom, for purposes of drainage. The gable end was habitually pressed into the hillside, thus presenting a further advantage in drainage. The older the site of a house, the more evident the native cunning which determined it. In the case of a longhouse, sometimes with a considerable extent of byre to the downhill side of the domestic accommodation, the building was planned to allow for efficient drainage.

The towns and villages were sited with the same care. Dolgellau, built up as a trading centre, still shows the pattern of its medieval

The farmhouse at Ty-isaf (right) demonstrates the scheme of digging one gable end back against the hillside, allowing for better drainage, and it uses the hill itself for shelter.

Ysgubor-newydd (below) is a good example of a boulder-built farmhouse in Snowdonia, keeping to the pattern of the longhouse in which the farmer and animals shared the same roof.

streets, a jig-saw puzzle for the traffic engineers but a visual delight, offering surprises and shifts of angle at every step. As the old, administrative centre it has invited waves of alteration, yet in total they add up to a remarkably homogenous whole tied together by the ubiquitous use of stone boulders. Ironically this scene, which strikes the visitor as so characteristically Welsh and obviously ancient, bears little resemblance to the buildings that would have stood in late medieval or Tudor Dolgellau. The house in which Owain Glyndwr (Owen Glendower) held a Parliament in 1405 still stood in the 1870s. Like many buildings of that period, it was a timber-framed, jettied building – much more on the model of the houses of the Marches, with stone used only for the gable walls and for the chimneys, which would have been added at a later date.

Dolgellau grew up at the intersection of various trading routes and serviced a large agricultural hinterland. Livestock markets, tanneries and businesses associated with every branch of local agriculture flourished. Added to this was Dolgellau's rôle as the administrative centre of the region and a centre for printing and the publishing of newspapers – Welsh language on the whole. Dolgellau today, with its eighteenth-century planned town square and Victorian villas for the retired and English visitors, as well as the humbler cottages snaking along the lanes and up the hills, is a cross-section of the development of a Wales long directed from England, but determined to be culturally separate from it.

The contrast with the slate industry towns a little further north is forcible. Although built in the local vernacular, it follows an industrial model constructed from immediately available materials. The cottages are of a standard terraced type and do not vary, except where they are affected by the lie of the land. Rising and falling with the landscape, sheer grey-black mountainside meeting the back walls, the terraces of the Welsh slate industry are tied to their former economic and geological *raison d'être*.

One of the points that gave slate its popularity over the long-dominant stone slates or roofing tiles in Britain was its lightness. Very thin by comparison with stone, it required a far less weighty substructure, allowing builders to use cheap softwoods for roof frames. It was also perfectly regular and therefore could be laid so that the roof surface was flush; stone slates were always irregular and thus had to be laid on a roof of much more acute pitch so that water would be thrown off. More shallow roofs suited the style of raised parapet which became popular in late eighteenth- and nineteenth-century terraced housing in particular. Finally, the fact that standard-size slate was laid in identical courses, rather than the diminishing courses of irregular slates, meant that roofing was far less highly skilled and a much less time-consuming operation. All these factors gave slate an unassailable head start countrywide over the attractive and traditional roofing materials.

Dolgellau is a town built of stone. Houses are constructed of boulders and roofed in slate. The house at the end of this lane is probably one of the earliest in the town to be built of stone. Surprisingly, this was once an area of timber-framed buildings.

These slate miners'
cottages in Blaenau
Ffestiniog (right) were
built in the standard
nineteenth-century
industrial terraced
pattern, utilising the
building materials to
hand; none nearer than
the sheer mountainside of
slate against which the
cottages are squeezed.

Tablets of slate like
this (below) are used as
fencing near Ffestiniog.
Wire is twisted between
them for reinforcement.

Slate is a reduced industry from its Victorian peak. The lament in *Old Cottages of Snowdonia* might be rephrased in contemporary terms to bemoan the replacement of slates with concrete tiles. The appalling conditions of the slate mines ensured that underground workings would eventually be closed. Now they are being reopened for the tourist, but the slate industry is booming.

Parallel with nineteenth-century development in the industrial towns and villages was a dramatic drop in population as the rural areas emptied to supply labour for the quarries and mines. Farms remained small, family operations on the whole, reflecting the established system in Wales of partible inheritance (as opposed to primogeniture). The drop in population, however, allied to continued agricultural prosperity with enlarged markets for wool and meat, allowed for a substantial rebuilding in the countryside. It was equivalent to the Great Rebuilding that had taken place in the seventeenth century in much of England. This led to the demolition of old houses, the incremental process of building on to and over earlier dwellings and the establishment of a more standardised though still vernacular style of building. The symmetrical gabled pattern established almost a century earlier still served its purpose, though the houses might be larger and the standard of domestic comfort considerably higher.

A field barn above Dolgellau is built of enormous boulders with a timber-framed interior. The barn exploits the change of levels. From this end the hay is pitched in to the cattle housed beyond at a lower level. The animals enter from the opposite end. This idea differs subtly in detail but reoccurs from one hilly area to another.

While the fortunes of those who mined the mountains for copper, slate or lead waxed and waned, those who depended on sheep experienced a less precarious existence. Even the small-scale, part-time farmer, a characteristic figure in this area, who combined a job as an artisan or tradesman with running a small flock of sheep, could manage a livelihood. Smallholdings still exist, sometimes preserving the range of traditional farm buildings longer than their grander neighbours simply because a single boulder-built barn-cum-byre might still be all that is needed for the enterprise. The open-sided hay barn, an indigenous building in north-west Wales, generally only appears on larger holdings but is a perfect example of the functional nature of farm buildings. A pitched slate roof supported on timber or, more rarely, slate posts, with solid gable ends, it is in fact the Dutch barn associated with arable areas – these days usually built in corrugated iron although the form was established as early as the late eighteenth century. Variations on this barn, with sections of wall broken by wide apertures or perhaps frequent air slits, are to be found all over the Snowdonia area. It is an essential building in a climate of so much rainfall, so little sun and relatively little wind. Hay was the one source of winter fodder on which the Welsh farmer could depend (the problems of arable cultivation were considerable), and so it was sufficiently important to merit this specific type of structure being developed in the late eighteenth, early nineteenth centuries. They have proved their worth and many remain in use.

The demolished Parliament house of Owen Glendower in Dolgellau gave way to a hardware store. The same family still remains in charge, and in the window is displayed the essential equipment for panning for gold. There is gold in these mountains, but not much of it. The hardware store offers no assurances of success in this enterprise. It is the short-legged, tough little Welsh hill sheep that have provided the gold in these mountains – the gold which built some of the finest early farmhouses in the country and sustained a way of life against adverse odds for hundreds of years. The terrain, climate and remoteness have placed obstacles in the way of both settlement and prosperity: it has been the sheep which have turned those impediments into advantages.

Tyddyn-y-felin, a farmhouse in the hills near Llanbedr, lies in a hollow, identifiable from a distance by its massive chimney stacks. Originally with a screens passage, it is a T-shaped house, a characteristic plan in this part of north-west Wales. It has a datestone of 1592.

Pennines: Bowland

Downham in
Lancashire is a stone-
built estate village in the
Ribble Valley.

Few areas of the British Isles can have so utterly escaped disfigurement at the hands of past or present generations as the small pocket to the west of the central Pennines known as the Forest of Bowland. This upland landscape, with lush, easy-going valleys giving way to harsh, rigorous fellside, has a population which has determined not to be imprisoned by its past, but has achieved a strong measure of continuity through it. The reasons are simple. The majority of people follow a way of life still concerned with the same things: conversation is of weather, market prices for sheep and cattle, village comings and goings. The buildings are the visual parallel to this, for they, the sturdy and functional houses and farm buildings, describe needs and processes which have altered little in two centuries.

The remoteness in this area on the Lancashire/Yorkshire border has had its own rewards. Visitors hurry northwards to the Lake District or eastwards to the Yorkshire Dales; there is too much fine scenery to go round. Travellers have always tended to miss the area. Even royalty, local landowners from 1399, found it too far from the beaten track to make much use of their deer parks and this disinterest allowed the Master Foresters to pursue their own advantages little troubled by outside interference. Lancaster, to the north west via the steep gorge of the Trough of Bowland, was the nearest city of importance. Burnley and Blackburn were, and still are, another world. Allegiances

From the rear, Harrop Hall wears a late eighteenth-century dress which has little in common with its front (see page 126 and page 152). The block in the centre background is in fact the earliest part of the house – the cross wing – now no longer used but readily identified by its chimney.

Stakes (right), built in 1613, is one of the first generation of fine stone-built gentry houses in the Forest of Bowland. Its site on the banks of the River Hodder was one of the best available in an area where the forest was being gradually pushed back. The wooded valleys are all that remain of the great woods. Like the other houses of its type, it has a fine oak roof frame.

are instead to the market towns – Clitheroe, Bentham, Gisburn or Skipton remain the local points of reference beyond the immediate area of the Hodder Valley.

This isolation has conspired to allow the Bowland area to progress at its own pace, hardly touched by revolutions of industry and agriculture, a fact which has led to a remarkable degree of self-contained prosperity. Railway and road transport, EEC subsidy and vast improvements in the material aspects of life have been assimilated but they have not disturbed the balance. Jobs still centre on agriculture (though increasingly on the service end of farming), work on the estates, in forestry or for the water authority; life is still based on the land, though the emphasis has shifted.

The buildings of village, hamlet and fellside are of stone – durable and sensible to the climate and the requirements of humans and animals. The structures of the area, from the sizeable 'gentry houses' of the western valleys to the rudimentary dry-stone walls snaking across the flanks of the fells, are homogenous and sternly beautiful. There are, of course, cracks in the varnish of this picture. The continuing tendency to farm amalgamation leads to redundant buildings. The pristine appearance of estate villages such as Downham and Slaidburn has been bought at the expense of neighbouring, less-protected villages. Sometimes unwordly estate management has set up its own problems. In Slaidburn, the united front of neat eighteenth- and nineteenth-century cottages and farm buildings that line the main street hides the problems of an estate which is adjusting

The last remaining fishermen's cottages are to be found on the quayside at **Kirkcudbright** in Scotland. Behind them is the town's high street, which follows the higher ground parallel to the estuary of the River Dee.

Dry stone walls, or drystane dykes as they are known in Galloway, snake across the moors beside the Old Military Road which runs from Creetown to Gatehouse. Boulders of granite litter the hillside and so are readily to hand.

The old grammar school at Slaidburn (below), endowed in 1717, is a fine stone building with sandstone mullioned and transomed windows. In the nineteenth century, the first floor was removed so that the present day primary school now has a full-height hall.

the balance following an era of somewhat misguided benevolence in which rents were artificially kept at a low level.

However, contrary to the over-riding impression of virtual change-lessness, the Bowland area did once, for a hundred years or so, witness a dramatic upheaval in which its landscape, agriculture and patterns of population were transformed. From a forested area, with small clearings and a large amount of scrub good for little except hunting, it became a prosperous pastoral neighbourhood. Farmland became available and the population rose accordingly. Its crude timber buildings went, replaced by solid, well-appointed stone ones. A society governed by the rules and regulations of forest authorities turned into an independent yeomanry and the population almost doubled. In 1500 this process of change had hardly begun; by 1650 it was complete. However, in the late medieval and early Tudor periods, the landscape was dominated by the great blanket of the Forest of Bowland. Though already depleted and intermittently punctured by areas cleared for pasture, the woodland swaddled the valleys and lower slopes of the fells. Hamlets, usually commemorating the sites of vast thirteenth-century oxen-raising ranches, consisted of ramshackle, often crudely constructed buildings of timber, mud and thatch. These were repaired, rebuilt or abandoned depending on the changing scene.

From the humblest shed to the grandest barn, the skeleton for all buildings was the cruck, A-shaped, consisting of paired timbers erected at set intervals, or bays. (There might be only one or two bays in humble buildings and as many as ten bays (eleven pairs of crucks) in the grander houses, such as Leigh Court in Worcestershire. Stonyhurst barn, a magnificent example in the Ribble Valley, has five pairs of crucks.) The big timbers making the sloping sides of the 'A' were elbowed at the three-quarter point to allow more room inside and each pair had to be carefully matched. The matching was often achieved by splitting a single log lengthwise into two, the choice of a suitable log being a matter of careful judgement. At the apex, where the paired timbers joined, there was usually a small crosspiece or yoke just below the ridge pole. Further horizontal posts, called purlins, ran at intervals below. Potentially the roof could virtually shroud the entire structure, tea-cosy fashion, but for practical reasons – of ventilation and light sources in particular – the gable walls were not sufficient and the windows and doors could be punched through the infilling material – wattle and daub or stone – between the crucks. Although the walls were always to remain structurally subservient to the roof structure, a further adaptation of the cruck frame was developed, the upper cruck, so that the walls at least shared the burden. In this case, there was an added advantage, for the collar and tie beam could be introduced higher up and an upper room with considerable head-room was gained. At a time when full-height rooms were being floored over, the upper cruck suited the new domestic arrangement well.

The cruck frame, like the other versions of timber-framed buildings, was assembled on the ground, pinned together with wooden pegs, and then reared and slotted together. It is a very different concept from masonry construction.

The advances being made in the rich south-eastern counties of England took a long time in reaching the remote north west, and the sophisticated dwelling of the Kentish yeoman farmer, for example, had no peer here. The cruck frame tended to prolong the life of the single-cell hall house – it certainly did not lend itself to the subdivisions that the box frame did.

By the late sixteenth century, timber in the Bowland area was becoming scarce and the best wood was prohibitively expensive. The remaining woodland was largely made up of saplings and scrub, of little use for building. Those who had administered the deer parks and been responsible for maintaining the forest had done little to prevent encroachment; they were amassing sizeable estates themselves and the economic stability of the Tudor era encouraged the professional classes and independent farmers to seek prosperity in the land. The most lucrative business, therefore, was to be had in helping them achieve their object.

The great barn at Stonyhurst in Lancashire (right) is one of the finest examples of Pennine cruck-frame construction. It is proof that the area was once richly forested in oak. With its five pairs of full

crucks, it was originally a corn barn on a wealthy estate. Now stone walled and roofed, it would once have been thatched and walled with timber panels. The cruck blades meet at the ridge pole and are tied just below

with a collar, and below that with a tie-beam. The staggered purlins, on which the rafters rest, are trenched into the backs of the cruck blades.

The detail (top left) shows the cruck spur

pinned into the blade with wooden pegs. It is likely that a wall post is embedded within the present walls.

Full height crucks were the grandest form of this type of timber framing. In the case of

less high quality wood, the cruck might be made in two sections, jointed, or here in the Pennines, the crucks confined to the upper part of the building – known as an upper or half cruck (above left).

Hacking Hall (above) shares with Hammerton Hall a profusion of gables and mullioned windows. Here, seen from the rear, is one of the two vast chimney stacks which heated the principal rooms in the house. The main entry, on the symmetrical façade (not pictured), was a porch on the angle between the main block and the projecting wings. To even things up, a matching bay was added, though it was not strictly needed.

The limited supply of timber coincided with a sudden demand for new buildings; a rapidly expanding population needed resilient, well-constructed houses and farm buildings. The first generation of stone houses was the furthest from the fells: they were the large 'gentry houses' of the newly rich professional classes, men who could afford the cumbersome business of bringing the limestone and local sandstone (mill-stone grit) down to the valleys. The example set in these large houses was soon followed by the next generation of smaller, fellside farmhouses whose masons were by now able to translate the elegance of the larger houses to their humbler relations.

The style of life of the confident, wealthy men who ran affairs in this part of the country was domestic in its emphasis. It was far from the embattled atmosphere in which the lawless clan, the Talbots, lived in Bashall Hall at the end of the fifteenth century, their own militia housed in barracks alongside. By 1607, when Judge Walmsley built Hacking Hall nearby in the Calder Valley, he was happy to provide attics for his retainers who were no longer a private army but merely employed to make such a house run smoothly. Hacking, like Stakes, on the Hodder, or Hammerton Hall nearer the head-waters of the same river, had all borrowed certain elements of the design of the great houses of the aristocracy or court favourites. Hammerton Hall, probably dating from the late sixteenth century, contains a magnificent stone spiral staircase and follows the E-plan of great Tudor houses with its entrance via a gabled, three-storey

Hammerton Hall is a fine example of the stone, multi-gabled mansions built for the gentry at the turn of the sixteenth century in the Forest of Bowland.

porch. Stakes, in common with Hacking, has a fine oak roof frame, using the cruck form of construction, proving that when the money was available to buy best oak, the carpenters still knew of no better system. But, despite such remnants of old skills, these houses were utilising new abilities. The load of the roof structure was now borne by stone walls, and all the finer details – mullioned and transomed windows, drip moulds and ornamented lintels, corbels and fine, closely pointed ashlared stonework – were the touches of men who were becoming well versed in the arts of stone masonry. Carpentry skills were evident in the panelling, stairs and fine oak floorboards.

Builders of smaller houses, such as Harrop Hall or Higher Stoneybank, both farms on the line between pasture and fell above Slaidburn, borrowed and scaled-down these details. Harrop has mullioned windows and the characteristic, rather later, ornamented and dated door lintel that is to be found on almost every seventeenth- and eighteenth-century house in the region. Higher Stoneybank, simple enough in its pedigree and scale to retain the cross-passage of a basic two-roomed house, still follows the example of the larger houses with its gabled porch. Here the farm buildings are under the same roof-line, though with separate entry, a feature often met with in Pennine areas and known, in Yorkshire at least, as the laithe house.

While the grander houses were spacious enough to devolve the various household activities to different parts of the house, the builder of the smaller farmhouse positioned the few rooms to make best use

Higher Stoneybank (left) and Harrop Hall (below left) are examples of seventeenth-century fellside farmhouses.

of all natural advantages – in particular aspect and location. The kitchen, dairy and pantry were always to the north, where possible the north east. Here slate surfaces, stone flagging and minimal light all helped to keep the temperature low. Living quarters were positioned to catch all available sunlight and natural warmth and to avoid the sights, sounds and smells of the adjacent farmyard. By the seventeenth century, solidly built chimneys were an important feature and a tax was levied on the number of hearths to a house.

Despite inclement conditions, the seventeenth- or eighteenth-century farmer had to put a fair proportion of his land down to arable cultivation. The survival of his family and livestock over the winter months depended on stocks of non-perishable foodstuffs, and oats were the most important of these. When in the nineteenth century transport and ready-made foodstuffs became available, the arable acres could revert to grass, though in twentieth-century wartime the process was once again reversed. A legacy of the arable acres on every farm is some kind of granary, secure from vermin, and a kiln, usually slatted wood over charcoal, with which to counteract the damp.

The field barn with shippon (below) marks the outer limits of pasture. The dry-stone wall snakes over the valley as a reminder of enclosures. Its construction depends on using stones of graduated size and staggering the joints. Larger stones, known as 'through stones', are laid transversely, at intervals.

The most perfectly functional of Pennine farm buildings, often still in use exactly as designed two hundred or so years ago, is the barn-cum-shippon. Here the cattle are tied in rows, facing on to a feeding passage and backing on to a cleaning passage. A low ceiling, stacked above with the supply of hay for the winter, which can be forked down through traps to the feeding racks below, allows for warmth.

The animals stand close together and the ventilation, through narrow slits in the thick rubble walls, is sufficient but allows little heat loss. On the coldest nights the cattle are snugly cocooned.

While cattle, and calves, required good, weather-proof buildings, sheep had few requirements. A few solid walls and, occasionally, some dry-stone pens, gave the sheep sufficient shelter in all weathers, though in the past, as now, they were brought down from the more exposed fellsides at the onset of bad weather.

Some farms produced cheese, traditionally the province of the farmer's wife, but on a limited scale. When self-sufficiency was the keynote of existence in these remote areas, the fine balance between the number of animals kept and the amount of fodder needed for their survival could be easily tipped by a hard or long winter. Acreage per farm was small and the number of animals severely limited by that; one of the major changes of the last thirty years has been one of scale, both in farm size and the number of livestock held.

Sites for farmhouses were carefully chosen, usually in a sheltered fold in the ground and close to water. Similarly the outbarns were sited as they were required, far out on the most exposed points of fellside pasture. Nowadays, when derelict, they provide an indication of how far up towards the moors the limits of pasture extended at a time when every acre was in demand. With enclosure of the common lands, the walls marked out the farmer's land and these remain as evidence of eighteenth- and nineteenth-century farming enterprise. Often one barn served each grazing area, though they are not as ubiquitous as the tiny field barns that dot the Yorkshire Dales further east. The proximity of the barn to the hay fields was of course convenient at hay-making time of year, while the constant problem of high rainfall meant that heavy eaves and a protected canopy or porch allowed the loaded carts or sleds to shelter in sudden summer storms. Barns in the farmyard itself had details such as pitching holes and were close to the midden, so that manure could be easily cleared out of the shippons and put to good use.

As building continued at a constant pace through the seventeenth, eighteenth and early nineteenth centuries, so quarries and lime kilns came to pock-mark virtually every fellside. Lime was burnt for mortar and as fertiliser, and the limestone and sandstone dictated their own best use. Limestone, friable and less satisfactory than sandstone, was used in rubble walling, infilling and sometimes for the dry-stone field walls. The best quality free-stone (so-called since it could be laid any way up, not just on its natural bed) was used for the door and window lintels and jambs, for quoins, important elevations and for the best quality dry-stone walls. Since the Bowland area has frequent outcrops of limestone interrupting the prevailing geology of millstone grit, the two could be economically used in combination.

All over the Pennines the availability of good-quality building stone and the energies of local farmers combined to develop a rich

This milestone (left) near Newton marks the direction along fellside tracks. The tracks were hard to find, and even harder to follow, in Pennine winters.

The chiselled gatepost (right) is at Halstead, one of the few farms which did not disappear when the parish of Dalehead, beyond Slaidburn, was flooded in the 1920s to provide the Stocks Reservoir.

vernacular architecture. It arose in response to need and was based on traditional skills which had little in common with the academic and intellectual pursuits of professional architects. Yet, despite the identical needs of upland farming throughout the area and the similarities of climate, each area – even each Dale – had its own peculiar details. Only a little further east, in the Yorkshire Dales, or north west in the Lake District barns were built using the fall in the ground to best advantage; hay was forked in at a higher level, whilst the cattle entered, from the other side, at the lower level. Just as dialect changed from place to place, so these small adaptations remained highly localised – the trademark of one valley and its people.

The development of the villages followed that of the hamlets and outlying farmsteads. There many of the population combined farming with a second activity, most commonly the fulling of woollen cloth. Sheep had provided much of the wealth of the Pennines from the Tudor period onwards and with industrialisation the fast running streams could be put to good use. Slaidburn, for example, although prosperous enough to house a church furnished with superb oak carvings, pews and a three-decker pulpit, and to pride itself on the fine grammar school, endowed in 1717 and functioning now as the village primary school, had a boom in the late eighteenth and early nineteenth centuries. The village shifted eastwards to realign with the roadside, leaving the site of the medieval village which had been alongside the Hodder, south of the church. Here terraces of simple two-storey cottages, built of local stone constructed in a particular waterproof system (water coursing, consisting of slightly overlapping and sloping stonework) are a sign of this new source of prosperity. Many of the farms were part of this pattern, the house and barn facing on to the road, the remaining farm buildings tucked around at the back. In 1844 there were thirteen farms within the village, forty-four more in the parish area. In Slaidburn in the early 1980s four farms are active within the village itself and a handful outside.

After this period of expansion, Slaidburn and the surrounding area settled down. Its population was established, its way of life rarely interrupted. The devastating agricultural slump, which hit the arable counties of the eastern parts of England and Scotland in the late nineteenth century, had little effect on these upland pastoral farming areas. When in the late 1920s, the Fylde Water Authority dammed the upper waters of the Hodder to form the Stocks Reservoir, which flooded the remote hamlet of Dalehead, it proved impossible to find masons or quarrymen in sufficient numbers locally to construct the dam and associated new buildings from local stone. Dozens of skilled men were brought in from outside the area, in particular from North Wales. Ironically, in this area once cleared back from forest, the old farms of Dalehead which fell within the catchment area of the reservoir were to become sterilised land, used for forestry.

Skills in the use of stone which the seventeenth- and eighteenth-century population had learned as they built and rebuilt for their needs, had remained untapped since then. While every farmer could lay a dry-stone wall, observing its basic structural principles in order to build a wall which would last a generation – and many still can – the more specialist masonry skills, once so abundant, had gone. In this solidly constructed and well-maintained area there really was nothing more to be done.

Nowadays, in a region dominated by stone, outcropping on the hills and fells, exposed in innumerable disused quarries, where parish boundaries and field edges are marked by boulders and where every house, barn and stretch of wall is of the local rock, there is a desperate need for skilled stone masons. Now when barns are converted, local builders encrust the surface with ribbons of mortar, obscuring the old, razor-sharp and discreet pointing with great worms of cement. Bottle glass and bow windows, frosted glass panels in place of tongue-and-groove wooden doors, bleak panes of double glazing in place of glazing bars or even mullions, Gothic iron hinges, handles and nailheads in place of simple detail – all have crept in here and there. The estates, from the largest to the smallest, are generally conscientious landlords, careful to preserve the architectural integrity of the area in which they have the good fortune to have a stake. The beauty of this built landscape depends less on the particular than on the general abundance of congenial architecture, a tribute to the fine local stone, traditionally used with competence and artistry.

The main street of Slaidburn is lined with solid terraced cottages of eighteenth and nineteenth century date. They point to the importance of a village as the centre for a large and scattered rural area. All the local tradesmen, joiners, tailors and shoemakers would have lived in the village, servicing the outlying farms and hamlets. The cobbled pavements are reminders of the days before tarmac and motor transport.

Galloway

Rusco is a mid fifteenth-century tower house in the Galloway town of Gatehouse of Fleet.

In that corner of south-western Scotland which points a set of pudgy, finger-like peninsulas at the English coast across the Solway, is one of the oddest landscapes to be found anywhere in Britain. Inland the scene is a recognisably Scottish one: low hills rolling to a chain of mostly granite mountains, intersected by wide and frequent valleys. On the tips of these 'fingers' the terrain looks as though a green baize cloth has been dropped over a heap of potatoes. This knobbly, awkward landscape is the result of glacial moraine, deposited in the wake of the Ice Age. Such a primeval landscape must have proved rather unnerving for early settlers to the area, so they directed their attention to the valleys and the infrequent calmer stretches of ground for the location of the characteristic 'fermtoun' or group of farm-steads.

This inhospitable and remote landscape ensured that it was rela-tively unvisited except from the sea. Nordic invaders came in the ninth century and, together with the native Gallovidians, they made up a Gaelic-speaking population, in contrast to the more eastern Border country where that tongue and culture made little or no impression. Gaelic was still spoken in Galloway, at least in the re-moter parts, in the late sixteenth century.

This long history of sparse settlement and separateness infected the view English visitors held of the area; writers of the eighteenth- and nineteenth-centuries tend to describe the manners and habits of the natives of the region in a condescending tone similar to that which they applied to Ireland. Much was made of the languor of the people, their poverty and the unfair advantages taken of them by some of their landlords. There were no roads, for example, except for the drovers' tracks, until the military road was pushed through from Newton Stewart to Dumfries after the '45 Rebellion. Daniel Defoe visited Kirkcudbright a few years after the Act of Union between England and Scotland (1707) and wrote: 'Here is a pleasant situation, and yet nothing pleasant to be seen. Here is a harbour without ships, a port without trade, a fishery without nets, a people without business ...' Modern Kirkcudbright, the most ancient town on this coast, could hardly present a more different picture – the very model of an attractive, historic town which has preserved its charms whilst attaining considerable prosperity.

As in much of Scotland, the built landscape of Galloway, and in particular the Stewartry of Kirkcudbright (so-called since the chief official of the county was a Steward) is a relatively recent one. Towns such as Castle Douglas, Gatehouse of Fleet or Newton Stewart bear the marks of being planned as a whole: they are roadside settlements with a homogenous style of building which makes them seem more urban and sophisticated than they can ever have been in the past. By the middle of the eighteenth century there had been virtually no development in domestic architecture since the late-medieval fortified tower house. That structure, a symbol of the landowning class, remained a fit establishment for men who were constantly threatened by the English, their neighbours or their tenants. At the foot of these towers were the miserable, single-room dwellings of the peasantry. Thatched with heather, ferns, broom or straw and walled with granite boulders taken off the ground nearby, or even with packed clay, they must have been similar to the Hebridean or Highland blackhouse as it has survived into the present century. It was as if the medieval fortified manor of southern and central England and the primitive timber and clay huts of the landless labourers had been the sole development in building until the eighteenth century. The dramatic improvements in domestic architecture which took place in the sixteenth and seventeenth centuries in most of England and parts of Wales, even in the most culturally and geographically remote of areas, had no parallel in Scotland. The jump from the late medieval period to the eighteenth-century, classically influenced architecture of town and village was a sheer leap.

The most obvious reason seems to be the continual state of political and economic uncertainty between the nations facing one another across the Solway, reinforced by the threat of actual violence. On the English side of the border, Northumberland shows all the same signs and also has a similar historical gap between the fortified pele tower and the orderly villages and farmhouses of the late eighteenth and

This harled farmhouse surrounded by dry-stone walls is on the coast near Auchenlarie. Harling is the Scottish equivalent of rendering.

early nineteenth century. It was the imposition of the new enclosed landscape upon Scotland that led to the final spate of disruption – the civil disorder of a group known as the Levellers, who protested against the tenants' loss of grazing rights on the landlords' lands, the raising of dry-stone walls (or dykes) across the open moorland and, worst of all, the loss of small crofts by amalgamation into larger farm units. The Levellers, who rose in the Kirkcudbright area in the mid 1720s, worked in groups, flattening the walls as they were built. Finally they were rounded up, fined, imprisoned or, in some cases, deported. The landlords proceeded with the formation of the land-scape we know today.

Kirkcudbright itself is something of an exception. Built originally in an L-shape, the houses lining its high street were the solid seventeenth-century town houses of a merchant class or, in some cases, of the landowners who otherwise inhabited those secure towers out in the open countryside. Although elegant eighteenth-century town houses mostly replaced these gabled, rubble-walled houses, a few still remain – huddled around the Tolbooth, a sixteenth-century town hall-cum-gaol in which was imprisoned, amongst others, John Paul Jones. The pattern preserved by these houses, with their steep roof pitches as a reminder of the fact that they were originally thatched, was the practice of building gable-end on to the street. This

This view of Kirkcudbright is from the roof of the courthouse. The building in the centre is the Tolbooth. Next to it is a seventeenth-century town house, gable end on to the street and extending back in a series of blocks, each one lower than the one before. Each pair of houses is separated by a close. Long gardens extend to the River Dee behind.

was economical of building land which was severely limited by the fact that much of the land was on a flood plain. The high street represented a gravel ridge, out of harm's way. This arrangement, giving a limited street frontage, means that the houses are developed in a series of backward steps – dropping in height all the time. The effect is like a set of children's building bricks, a neat sequence of gable upon gable. Stables or outbuildings form the lowest block in the stack with the gardens beyond that. The houses were reached by means of closes or wynds running between them, providing access for each pair of neighbours and leading to the thin garden strips (long lots) and drying greens for laundry beyond. On the north-western side of town the houses and gardens ran directly down to the banks of the River Dee. The best view of this pattern is obtained from the site of the one remaining working yair net, used for salmon, on the opposite bank. There, a form of fishing in which the fisherman operates the net through his fingers, while sitting on a flimsy platform over the water as perfected by pre-Dissolution monks and now solely practised here, is carried out against the background of Kirkcudbright ancient and modern. Ancient with the silhouette of a ruined castle (home of the MacLellans) and Tolbooth (home of the coastguard service these days), modern with the thriving fishing industry which has returned to the town in the last decade thanks to the discovery of a small scallop, known as a 'queenie', found off the coast here and the energies of a local fisherman turned entrepreneur.

Travellers had long noted the attractive closes behind the old houses in Kirkcudbright and it was this feature, together with the quality of the light, that established the town as an artists' colony in the early years of this century when young painters from Glasgow and Edinburgh settled here. The setting was also caught by Dorothy Sayers as the background for her detective novel, *Five Red Herrings*, in which her hero Lord Peter Wimsey tirelessly travels the road between Gatehouse of Fleet and Kirkcudbright in search of clues. She also uses the fact that the mountainsides to the north are pock-marked with disused lead mine shafts and overgrown quarries, commemorating the natural resources which made Galloway rich and famous in the eighteenth and nineteenth centuries.

Building materials were traditionally the igneous whinstone, found widely in the locality, the red sandstone, which was brought in from the Dumfries district and, in the nineteenth century, granite. Good timber was hard to find west of Dumfries. Suiting the Victorian builder's desire for durability and neatness, the new town houses were granite-walled with their sills, lintels and quoins of the more malleable sandstone. Granite could be split – a skilful mason would know how to find any weakness – but it was with mechanisation that it became more widely used as a building stone, for cladding and for monumental masonry, in other parts of Britain and the Empire.

Ironically enough, the granite setts which went from the Creetown quarry (still operational) to build the Merseyside Docks, have recently returned to base to be cut down further and used for other purposes – these days most likely as memorials. Creetown Granite, in a brochure produced in the late 1920s, described the market for its product, built up in the preceding eighty years of operation. It had been chosen for memorials 'to be shipped to all quarters of the Globe: the Colonies, China, North and South America, Sumatra, wheresoever the ubiquitous Scot is to be found'. In addition, it was used for 'modern Business Building Fronts' as for paving stones and setts. Recently granite has been available more cheaply from India, South Africa or Scandinavia and the cladding of a new generation of office blocks usually returns by the same route as it was once exported.

Happily, Scottish granite is again becoming more competitive and is being used more widely for cladding. Nevertheless, as a building stone it is an anachronism – the chiselling of heavy blocks and careful pointing, enlivened traditionally with 'snakes' of whinstone chips, is not a labour for a modern builder. The houses that line the streets of Creetown, Dalbeattie (another quarry town) or Newton Stewart may not be of great age, probably most have been built within the last century, but they are relics of a redundant skill. That granite only appears now in the graveyard or buried deep beneath the tarmac is an appropriate metaphor for its fate in the building industry. The oldest houses in the region, the tower houses or castles, such as Rusco, outside Gatehouse, Cardoness, Carsluith or Barholm along the coast towards Newton Stewart, or the splendid Hills Tower further east near Dumfries, were built of a mixture of stone, used without regular coursing, as a rubble walling finish. Though Rusco was converted to a house once again in the 1970s, most of them have remained derelict. At Hills Tower, which dates from 1528, with a gatehouse and a farmhouse dated 1721, the pattern emerges clearly. The Tower, encircled by its barbican wall and miscellaneous farm buildings (the latter gone long since), would have provided accommodation on three levels, with space for cattle, if needed, below. The

Hills Tower at Lochfoot (right) is a tower house. It is rare in retaining the barbican wall and gatehouse (below). As one of the last generation of tower houses, it is less overtly offensive than Rusco, built a century earlier. The section through the tower house (below right) shows how it is little more than a tall square house built of massively solid masonry.

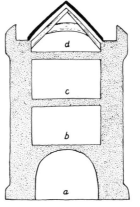

The vaulted undercroft (a) was a storage space, the two intervening floors (b and c) were the living accommodation, and the upper storey (d) was a garret.

Granite block interspersed with whinstone chips (above) is a local technique known as 'snakes'.

house, early in date in these regions for such a symmetrical, classical type of house, then took over the functions of the tower. Similarly, at Carsluith, the farmhouse and outbuildings of the late eighteenth or early nineteenth century flank the tower, by then nothing but a picturesque ruin. At Barholm, the tower, and a good deal of the lower walls of an adjacent building of the same date, stand in the midst of a farmyard with a typical eighteenth-century farmhouse alongside.

The oldest of the next 'generation' of houses in this area built for what were known as 'pocket lairds' – yeoman farmers, in fact – is Barmagachan, outside Borgue, south-west of Kirkcudbright. Here the characteristic steep roof pitch, rubble walls and crow steps show it to be a house of the early eighteenth century. The stepped gables, much more common on the eastern coast of Scotland, are both an aesthetic touch and a practical one, throwing rainwater off the coping and away from the walls. Here, in an area with a high rainfall, although always warmed by the Gulf Stream, that is an important consideration. Another house with a similar air, although a little closer to the classical simplicity of a mid-eighteenth-century farmhouse, is Kelton Mains, built in the 1720s. Its two curving walls, each tipped by a little pavilion, give it a French look. Originally it was a double-pile house, with a similar block to the present house joined on to the back.

Despite this move towards symmetry, and the string of elegant, architect-designed lairds' houses that appeared in the area once all was peaceful, there was still plenty of evidence of earlier discomfort. In his *Journey through Scotland* (1793), Robert Heron noted farmhouses which he described as 'very unpretending and uncomfortable erections. The dwelling-house, byre and stable usually formed one building of low elevation, popularly known as the "long range". Sanitary arrangements which are now so much attended to, were never considered worthy of a thought.' Nevertheless, the new, enclosed landscape had dictated a neat approach to building which was soon as much the vernacular of south-western Scotland as had been the rude huts of earlier times.

The small houses, two or even one-and-a-half storeys, replaced the longhouses or the 'but and ben' arrangement of simple cottages – the but was the kitchen and living area, the ben the best room. There was often a sleeping lobby between the two. Gabled dormers, sash windows, a neat gabled porch and slated roof were the norm, all set, where possible, to face the south. Traditionally, for reasons of sheer common sense, the rest of the steading – the byres, stables, barns and later the engine or wheel-houses of mechanised agriculture – were tacked on the back of the house to its north face. There, for practical reasons, the dairy and kitchen-pantry could be usefully sited; it was cool and the farmer's wife could feed the pigs with the whey from the dairy, and the poultry with the peelings from the kitchen. Every farm made its own cheese.

At Cardoness this tiny double cottage is of the type known as 'but and ben'. It is ornamented with a Gothic chimney pot and latticed windows to give it the distinguishing marks of an estate cottage.

Farming, carried out by tenants of the large and often ancient estates in this part of Scotland, was and remains predominantly pastoral, with some arable on the kinder stretches of the valleys. Along the Dee, for instance, the farms are much closer in type to those of eastern Scotland than to the little upland farms of the extremities of the Solway estuary or on the higher ground behind. Sheep and cattle graze together, with the belted Galloway and Ayrshire cattle now sharing their patch with the ubiquitous Friesian or Charolais. Those farmers whose lands border the Dee share the

The back of Glentoo farmhouse has the characteristic outshot which originally housed the dairy and perhaps a pantry for food storage. Whitewashed rubble and a tiled roof are typical building materials for farmhouses such as this one. This farm still retains the circular wheelhouse for powering a threshing machine turned by horse or donkey.

privilege of being the proprietors of the yair net downstream at Kirkcudbright, whilst along the coastline stand the stake nets, complex trapping systems which, when they are not in use, look like some mysterious slalom course. Stake netting salmon is another traditional occupation here, carried on seasonally and alternated with such occupations as those of jobbing builder or gamekeeper.

Slate, much of it brought in by water from Lancashire or Wales in the nineteenth century, is now the common roofing material, though there was also a local slate which took over from thatch in the same period. Eventually it proved too flaky and only imported slates were used. Nevertheless, since many of the tenants had been expected to build their own houses, it is not surprising that the cheapest, most easily obtained materials were used. Hence the constructions of flimsy timber, poor slates or mixed thatch, with rubble or even clay walls. The early longhouse, replaced by the standard nineteenth-century cottage, had started out without chimney or windows beyond mere shuttered slits. The longhouse in this primitive form disappeared when land was reorganized with parliamentary enclosure and the long traditional fermtoun disappeared to be replaced by the scattered, self-contained steadings of small- and medium-scale agriculture. The form nevertheless lived on; many of the new, neat farmhouses still abut a barn-cum-byre, or byre alone, reflecting the old practice more as a matter of habit than anything else. The two parts had long since ceased to interconnect and so the attachment was merely an historic memory.

Further up the scale, the larger steading always favoured the fashionable square layout, with farmhouse facing outwards and farmyard tucked in behind, and flanked by the full complement of functional farm buildings which respected the links between animals (via manure) and crops (as fodder, as well as fertilised land). The midden, into which manure was shovelled prior to being taken out onto the field, had a suitably central position in this arrangement. Once the grievances of the Levellers were forgotten, the Galloway area settled into a pattern of tenant farming that has continued to this day, with only marginal shifts when tenants buy their farms off the estates.

As the shape of the countryside changed from the more stable late eighteenth century onwards, so too did Kirkcudbright. The pattern of seventeenth-century houses was greatly enlarged, mostly through the efforts of the Selkirk estate, the largest of the local landowners. The town extended, keeping to the original L of the high street, completing the square and adding a cross-stroke or two. The tight grid imposed was not broken until late in the nineteenth century when detached villas began to straggle along the roads which led in from various directions. This coincided with the beginning of the end for Kirkcudbright as a flourishing port, particularly when the railway bypassed it: water-borne traffic continued to drop until a surprising reversal in the late 1960s when a fishing industry was revived and fish processing and packing became a large-scale business.

Kirkcudbright is here seen from the opposite bank of the River Dee. The harbour cottages in the centre are the last of the simple fishermen's dwellings in the town. Behind them is the ruined castle of the MacLellans.

Kirkcudbright, better than the rural areas around it, demonstrates a progressive shift in building practice towards a much more homogenous style, though it is architecture which still depended on the building materials to hand. True, if the local slates were poor quality, they were brought in across the water, but the skills of building still emerged from the demands of dealing with a limited range of available materials. Now that cheap, available materials are so unrelated to those formerly in use, it is no surprise that the skills are dormant, if not dead.

Glossary

Aisled frame One in which the main span of the building is separated by a range of timber posts and braces from the side aisles

Arcade post A timber between the main span and the aisle

Ashlar Blocks of masonry worked to a smooth, even face and square edges and then laid in horizontal courses

Baffle entry An entrance to a room from outside the house sited opposite the side wall of a chimney stack

Bonding Method of laying bricks. There are many different arrangements such as Flemish bond and English bond, where alternate courses are either exclusively headers (end face) or stretchers (side face)

Box frame Timber-framed construction where the roof trusses are carried by vertical and horizontal members

Brace A subsidiary timber to strengthen

Bressumer beam An exposed horizontal beam holding the upper floor in a timber-framed house

Byre Cattle shed

Capital The decorative head of a column

Clay bat (or lump) Large unfired bricks made of clay

Clunch Hard chalk used as a building material (particularly in Cambridgeshire)

Cob A walling material of clay mixed with straw and gravel or grit

Corbel A projection of stone or brickwork which supports a floor or roof

Crow steps Steps on the sloping sides of a gable

Course Arrangement in layers of stones or bricks where they are of uniform height

Cross-passage One that divides the house from the front to the back into domestic and service areas

Cruck frame Timber framing using pairs of large curved timbers, known as crucks, which rise from ground level to the apex of a roof and act as principal supports

Dais Raised platform denoting the dining area in a medieval hall. Sometimes demarcated by a dais screen

Double-pile plan A farmhouse plan which allows for four rooms on two floors; two at the front and two at the back

Dressing Prepared stones which provide a feature to door or window mouldings, dripstones, etc

Drip mould (dripstone, drip) A projecting moulding over windows and doors which protects the wall from rainfall

Flushwork Flint used with dressed stone to make a decorative pattern, e.g. inscriptions

Footing Base of brick or stone, used both for timber- and earth-walled buildings

Gable Vertical wall, generally triangular, at the end of a pitched roof (Dutch gables have curved outlines)

Galleting (or garretting, garnetting) Tiny pieces of stone, flint chips, etc, set into mortar when soft to give a decorative effect

Hafod A summer house for upland farming (Welsh)

Hall house Medieval house with the main room the full height of the house

Hammer beam A bracket, projecting horizontally at wall-plate level, which carries the arched braces and struts supporting the roof

Hendre The principal farmhouse on lower grounds (Welsh)

Herring-bone When bricks, tiles or stones are placed in a zig-zag pattern

Hipped roof A roof with sloping ends. Half-hipped roof is one in which the lower part is gabled and the upper part is hipped

Jamb The vertical side of a window or doorway

Jetty The upper floor overhang on a timber-framed building

King post A perpendicular beam in the frame of a roof rising full height from the tie-beam to the ridge

Laithe house A later version of the longhouse, combining house, barn and byre under one roof with doors to each from the outside. (Usually North country)

Lath A narrow sliver of timber used to provide a backing for plaster on walls

Linhay (linney) A West country building with an animal shelter on the lower level and an open-fronted upper level for hay, known as a tallet

Lintel A horizontal support bridging an opening, either a wooden beam or a large stone

Lobby entry A front entrance to a house which opens into a lobby opposite an axial chimney stack

Longhouse Farmhouse and byre under one roof separated by a through passage usually an entrance to both parts

Midstrey Central entrance bay of a threshing barn often with a projecting porch

Mullion A vertical subdivide (stone or wood) in a window

Newel post The main post at the end of a flight of stairs. It supports the handrail and strings

Oast house A structure to house the kiln for drying hops

Outshot (outshut) A roofed-over lean-to extension

Pantile Curved, S-shaped roof tiles which are easy to overlap while preserving ventilation

Pargetting Exterior plastering ornament, either incised or in relief

Pele (or peel) **tower** Small fortified tower found on both sides of the England/Scotland border

Pitching hole (or eye) Opening in a wall of a barn or loft for unloading straw, corn or hay, usually closed with a sliding or hinged shutter

Pound house Purpose-built structure housing a cider press in the West country

Purlin In a timber-framed building, a horizontal beam supporting the common rafters

Quoins Dressed stones or bricks laid at the corners

Random Not laid in courses

Rendering Coating of plaster or cement

Screen passage A cross-passage partitioned off by screens

Sett Granite paving block

Shippon A cow shed in the North country

Staddle stone Mushroom-shaped stones used to support granaries and designed to deter vermin

Strapwork A form of Jacobean decoration which resembles interlaced strips of leather or fretwork

Studs Vertical timbers in a timber-framed wall

Tallet see Linhay

Through stones Protruding masonry, especially in a drystone wall

Tie-beam The principal horizontal beam in a roof connecting the feet of the rafters. They are usually sited at wall-plate height

Tithe barn Large barn in which one-tenth of the farm's produce (the tithe) was stored. This levy was paid to the church

Tower house Scottish fortified dwelling (see pele tower)

Tracery The ornamental intersections in the top part of a window, particularly used in arches and vaults

Transom A horizontal subdivide to a window or panel

Truss The timbers which form a bracket or bridge a space in a building

Tumbling Triangular arrangement of bricks on end walls, chimney stacks and gables. By laying them at right angles to the slope of the roof there was a smooth edge to the coping

Wall-plate The longitudinally laid timbers upon which rest the ends of the rafters, and the verticals, posts and studs

Wattle and daub A medieval wall construction of interwoven sticks or wattle which is then plastered over with daub (clay or mud)

Wealden house A specific type of medieval timber-framed house with a central hall and a two-storeyed bay jettied at each end. The whole house is covered by a single roof structure

Weather stones Projecting stones on a chimney stack which guard the joints on a roof from water penetration

Wind-braced timbers These timbers strengthen the roof by increasing its resistance to wind pressure. They are set diagonally and are often curved

Valleys The junction of two roof surfaces, usually at right angles to each other

Bibliography

Barley, M. W. *The English Farmhouse and Cottage* Routledge & Kegan Paul 1961

Beresford, Maurice *The Lost Villages of England* Lutterworth Press 1954

Brown, R. J. *The English Country Cottage* Hale 1979; *English Farmhouses* Hale 1982

Brunskill, R. W. *Illustrated Handbook of Vernacular Architecture* Faber 1978; *Traditional Farm Buildings* Gollancz 1982

Clifton-Taylor, Alec *The Pattern of English Building* Faber 1972; *English Stone Building* (with A. S. Areson) Gollancz 1983

Darley, Gillian *The National Trust Book of the Farm* Weidenfeld and Nicolson 1981

Defoe, Daniel *A Tour Through the Whole Island of Great Britain 1724–7* Everyman's Univ. Library Dent 1975

Fenton, A. and Walker B. *Rural Architecture of Scotland* J. Donald 1981

Fiennes, Celia *The Illustrated Journeys of Celia Fiennes 1685–1703* Christopher Morris (Ed.) Macdonald 1982

Gotch, J. A. *Squires' Homes and Other Old Buildings of Northamptonshire* Batsford 1939

Harris, R. *Discovering Timber-framed Buildings* Shire 1978

Heron, Robert *Journey through Scotland 1793*

Hoskins, W. G. *The Making of the English Landscape* Hodder 1977; *Midland England* Batsford 1944

Hudson, W. H. *Afoot in England* Oxford Univ. Press 1982

James, Henry *English Hours* Leon Edel (Ed.), Oxford niv. Press 1981

Mercer, E. *English Vernacular Houses* HMSO 1975

Meredith, George *Diana of the Crossways* (1885) Virago 1980

Penoyre, John and Jane *Houses in the Landscape* Faber 1978

Pevsner, N. (Ed.) *The Buildings of England* Penguin (various dates)

Sandon, E. *Suffolk Houses: Study of Domestic Architecture* Baron Pub. 1977

The Shell County Guides Faber (various dates)

Smith, Peter *Houses of the Welsh Countryside* HMSO 1975

Whitaker, T. H. *History of Whalley* 1876

Yaxley, D. *Portrait of Norfolk* Hale 1977

Periodicals and papers used as source material by region

Kent
Traditional Kent Buildings no. 1 and no. 2: studies by students at the School of Architecture, Canterbury College of Art. Jane Wade (Ed.) Published by the college 1980 1981

Suffolk and Essex
Carpenter, R. *Pargetting* SPAB News vol. 4 no. 2 April 1983

Proctor, J. M. *East Anglian Cottages* Providence Press 1979

Traditional Building Materials in Essex no. 1 produced by Historic Buildings and Construction Dept. of Essex County Council

Devon
Devon's Traditional Buildings Devon County Council 1979 *Archaeology of Devon Landscape* ibid 1981 *Devon's Heritage: Buildings and Landscape* ibid 1982

Northamptonshire
Enticknap, J. and Keen, J. *Collyweston Slating* Heritage Outlook vol. 2 no. 3 May/June 1982

Pennines
Porter, J. *A Forest in Transition: Bowland 1500–1650* Transactions of the Historic Society of Lancashire and Cheshire vol. 125 1975 *Waste Land Reclamation in the sixteenth and seventeenth centuries: the case of south–eastern Bowland 1550–1630* ibid vol. 127 1978

Wales
Dolgellau Gwynedd County Council 1976

Hughes, H. H. and North, H. L. *Old Cottages of Snowdonia* 1908 Reprinted 1979 by the Snowdonia National Park Society

Scotland
Macloud, Innes F. *Old Kirkudbright* Old Galloway papers no. 1 Glasgow 1973

Norfolk
Mason, H. J. *Flint, the Versatile Stone* Providence Press 1978

Wright, A. *Flint Walling* SPAB News vol. 2 no. 4 October 1981

Yaxley, D. and Virgoe, N. *The Manor House in Norfolk* (a booklet in the Bygones series for Anglia Television) Boydell Press 1978

Author's Acknowledgments

For the past ten months I have been wearing two hats – as researcher for the Channel Four series *Built in Britain* and as author and contributory photographer for this book. This has allowed me the rare luxury, for a writer, of spending quite generous amounts of time in each of the eight areas of Britain covered in the book and to gain, as a result, a feeling of how past and present have come together in the buildings, expressed by life in and around them. Thanks are due to Artifax, the production company for the series and patient employers of an often elusive researcher. Jenny Reeks, Andrew Snell, Chris Goddard and Peter Middleton have all played a considerable part in the various stages of this book. In all these eight regions, and particularly in those with which I was least familiar, countless people have given their time and local knowledge with a generosity that never failed to astound. The list of names in full would be too long but I hope that all those owners and users of buildings mentioned here, the builders and buildings experts, and many others, will consider themselves included in these very sincere thanks. Some people, however, must be mentioned by name. In alphabetical order, they are: Gus Astley, Peter Beacham, Tom Collin, John Denny, Alfie Howard, Shawn Leavey, Tony Parkinson, John Penoyre, John Schofield, W. John Smith, David Stenning, David Yaxley. They all helped to point me in the right direction. If at any stage I have taken a wrong turning, I alone am to blame.

Several people have to work far harder than the author during the production period of a book. In this case, Charyn Jones, the editor, and Sally Smallwood, the designer, have done a fine job. Susanna Yager of Channel Four and Sara Drake of A.D. Peters, have both taken a constant interest in the project and, finally, to my patient household and friends, further thanks. G.D.

Picture Acknowledgments

All the photographs in this book are the work of the author Gillian Darley with the exception of those appearing on the following pages: p. 37 top, pp. 38-9, p. 40, p. 43, p. 44, p. 45, p. 47 by Ian Dobbie; pp. 58-9 by Michael Halford; half-title, p. 12 left, pp. 78-9, p. 80, pp. 82-3, p. 84, pp. 85, p. 88, p. 89, p. 92 by Neil Holmes; p. 37 bottom by Impact Photos/Alain le Garsmeur; p. 55 from the National Monuments Record; p. 71, p. 73, p. 77, p. 97, p. 106 by Andrew Snell; p. 7, pp. 48-9, p. 50, p. 52, p. 53, p. 54 by Pamla Toler. The illustrations are by Grant Morrison.

Index

The door to Harrop Hall, a fellside farmhouse in the Bowland area of the Pennines shows the ornamental lintel which carries the datestone and the initials of the owner.